"The Seventh Day is replete with ... of the never-ceasing abundance of our God! Within ... you will realize the power, provision, and proper perspective of how believers should honor our Lord with our talent, tabernacle, time, and testimony."

> ~ Pastor Nedra Buckmire
> ~Spirit and Truth Worship Center, Loganville G.A.
> Author of "Unlikely but Chosen."

"The Seventh Day will leave you optimistically offended, painfully propelled, while reigniting your audacity to hope in God again. This book is a must-read for professionals, students, theologians, scholars, seminarians, laymen and women, bible study groups, disciples, and new converts."

> ~Elder Judy Kirk, Grace Church International

"The Seventh Day takes you on a journey of the author's life that is full of zigs and zags. You will draw closer to God as you read about the many ways God reveals Himself as a provider, healer, and confidante."

> ~ Lydia Rose, Bereavement Specialist,
> Author of "Joy In Your Mourning."

"The Seventh Day is a personal, prophetic, purpose-driven account of the life experiences encountering God in His many characteristics. It will set a fire under faith as you begin to revisit the call, the purpose and the plan of God for your life."

> ~Sherry Davis, Financial Practitioner

" If you have ever been tempted to "help God" bring your vision to life, or wondered how to apply the promises of God to your life, The Seventh Day unlocks the mystery of how to access unlimited resources to experience all that God has provided."

> ~Felicia C. Johnson, 2018-2019 National President
> American Business Women's Association

The Seventh Day

Accessing Your Undeniable Resources to Experience the Promises of God

To Cousin Mae May God Continue to Bless You Always

Denise DeBurst Gines

The Seventh Day

Accessing Your Undeniable Resources to Experience the Promises of God

The Seventh Day shares personal stories of what it means to encounter God in His different characteristics.

DENISE DEBURST GINES

In Dedication and Appreciation

To my mother, Hattie, who taught me that I can do anything if I put my mind to it and always to find a reason to live life to its fullest.

To my brother: Andre, who is a support to me in my endeavors.

To my children, LeNeyce, Jamel, Will, and niece Tanji, who keep life from ever being dull or ordinary.

To my grandsons, Jahred, Aaron, and Taveion, who are my arrows shot into the future.

To my friends, who know me and still love me.

To readers: who will begin to access the undeniable resources and experience the promises of God in this Seventh Day.

In Loving Memory of
My Sister
Mary Lee Barnwell
And
My Daughter
Shakeema Cherise DeBurst

Contents

Part II: Adonai: "Lord, Master, or Owner"

Part III: El Shaddai: "Lord God Almighty"

Part IV: Yahweh (Jehovah): "The Most Sacred Name"

Part V: Yahweh Yireh (Jehovah Jireh): "The Lord Will Provide"

Part VI: Jehovah Nissi: "The Lord Is My Banner"

Acknowledgments

Thank you to my ride-or-die girlfriends, Beverly Gibson, Deborah Woods, Dorrie Michael, and Patricia Aiken, who hold up my arms when they get weary.

Cynthelia McIntosh, my sister-friend, who keeps me covered in prayer.

My sincere appreciation to:

Elder Judy Kirk, Lydia Rose, Marian Williams, and Sherry Davis for taking the time to read cover to cover and give feedback, encouragement, and endorsements.

Pastor Nedra Buckmire and Felicia Johnson for their heartfelt endorsements.

Fred and Mary Bondurant who give me refuge to recharge.

Roshon and Tony Thomas, of Maximmultimedia for social media and website management.

Special thank you to Bishop Johnathan and Dr. Antoinette Alvarado for bringing a clear and concise Spirit-filled Word each Sunday.

Introduction

Have you ever been somewhere and saw someone you knew and called out their name, but they didn't answer? You were sure it was them, so you call out again, but they still didn't acknowledge you. God has many names, and will always hear you call out. He wants us to experience His different characteristics by understanding what His names reveal. We may encounter Him as Yahweh, Adonai, Elohim, Jehovah Jireh, Jehovah Nissi, or El Shaddai.

Each name personifies a different aspect of his character. God created and completed His work by the seventh day, in doing so He provided every resource we need to be successful in living out our God given destiny.

We live in the Seventh Day, a day that is blessed and sanctified, where we only need to learn to access the undeniable resources that He has already provided. Once we understand that we are no longer in a day of waiting for things to happen to us, something powerful can happen through us. When we seek God's truth and desire to honor our covenant with Him, we have access to all of God's promises. God always fulfills His promises. He is simply waiting for you to call Him by name.

Imagine this, stopped at a red light, a truck pulls up next to me on the driver's side. I see the passenger side window of the truck come down, and the driver leans over to say something to me. I let my window down to hear what he is saying when I notice the side of the truck says, "Mercedes Auto Parts and Repairs." He tells me that he has a backlight component for my vehicle, and I should call the number on the truck.

The backlight of my car had blown out the day before. Fixing this situation should be easy, as I had done this before with another car I owned. At the Auto Zone Auto Parts store, I gave the technician the year, make, and model of my car, and he put it into the computer to see if they had the part in stock. Yes, they had it in stock. Then the bombshell, it would cost $238. "What?" I was confused. Maybe he misunderstood what I said I wanted. I repeated what part I wanted.

He said, "Yes, that is what it costs."

I said, "For a light bulb?"

The men in line behind me started smirking and eventually burst into belly roll laughter. The technician then explained that it wasn't only one bulb that was bad; it was the entire left-side backlight component. The men in the line were still laughing and now making remarks. "When you have a luxury car, then you have luxury car repair bills."

I left the store feeling confused. I am convinced that having my dream car was a desire of my heart orchestrated by God. One year for my birthday, my son gave me a 2005 C240 Mercedes Benz. I drove that car for many years without any significant problems. As the car got older, the repairs that were needed became costly. I was thankful for the fact that I had owned and driven the car of my dreams.

My grandson was turning 21-years old and needed a car desperately. He would receive the first installment of inheritance money I invested for him when he was five years old, and his mother passed away. As we began looking for a car, I envisioned the plan I had for him to maximize this funding. I shared this with him, and he agreed, but when we got to the car dealership, all bets were off. The car he purchased was nearly brand new and cost three times the amount we had agreed on. He was 21, and I wanted him to be happy. He was a hard and dedicated worker, who had to walk 7 miles home from work a couple of mornings after his car broke down.

Three days later, I receive a frantic phone call from my grandson. "Grandma, Grandma, I just had a head-on collision."

"Calm down," I tell him. "Are you alright?"

He tells me he is okay, merely rattled, but his car is totaled. He sent me photos. I was stunned. My friend, Deborah, was at my house. We jumped into her car and drove to the scene of the accident as fast as we could. It was hard to believe that he walked away from that mangled car.

Within three weeks, the insurance company paid us back almost everything we paid for the car. While we waited through the process, I had a rental car. Driving in my neighborhood, I passed the import car service shop, where I usually got my car oil changes and maintenance. As I passed by, I saw a for-sale sign on a vehicle in front of the shop. I made a U-turn and went back to the shop. There sat a beautiful Honda Accord with all the bells and whistles.

I called my grandson to tell him about it. He says that he believes that we should go back to the original plan and not spend so much on his car. I was so glad to hear that. I asked the owner of the shop the price of the vehicle. The price was 1/3 what he had paid for the totaled vehicle. My grandson came to test drive the car and decided to buy it.

While the paperwork was prepared, I told the owner that I, too, was looking to buy a car. He knew me well; after all, I visited the shop every 3000 miles for service. I was merely looking for a vehicle that will get me from point A to point B. He casually tells me that he will sell me the car that the shop uses as a loaner car. It was well maintained to ensure that while customers were having their car serviced that they could use a reliable vehicle with no worries.

I asked to see the car. It was sitting in front of the shop next to the Honda. When I went outside to see the car, I was shocked to see an E 330 Mercedes Benz. This automobile was a step up from my C230. It looked so good! The car was $2k more than I wanted to spend. I went home and did the research and determined that the vehicle was well worth the price.

The next thing I know, my grandson's friend, whose father is a mechanic, stopped by my house because his son told him I might want to sell the Mercedes Benz parked in my driveway. I told him what was wrong with the car, and he offered me $1500. What? $1500 for a car you have to tow out of my driveway? There was no hesitation. The E 330 was going to be mine.

Years later the backlight is the first issue I've had with this vehicle. What the man in the store said made sense, so I told God, "You never do things halfway. So if you gave me this car, you would give me what I need to maintain it as well." I had no car payment, so I was faithful to do the maintenance and to keep the vehicle clean.

I called the number on the side of the truck and made an appointment to go to his shop. When I left, I had a second-hand backlight component that I paid a total of $80 for, with labor. God showed up and let me know that He wasn't going to let me go backward. Though I was not even looking for another Mercedes Benz because I thought it would be impossible, He saw it fit that I go to the next level.

Though I've seen God move in different aspects of my life, I hadn't thought about the characteristics of God that I encountered. I began to acknowledge these encounters. They are encounters that blow me away, encounters that only He can orchestrate. I wanted to understand why God showed up the way he did in each encounter.

For instance, once, I stopped at Publix to pick up a few items for the Gilgal House, a women's shelter, in partnership with the women's ministry at my church. Several things the women's ministry would need for the fellowship were on sale. I grabbed the items that were buy-one-get-one-free and headed to the register. Once the cashier told me the total, I reached in my purse to realize I left my wallet with my debit card on the desk at home. I had some cash, but not enough for the total bill. I told the cashier that I would put back some of the items. She came on my side of the register and took out her credit card and swiped it for the balance. She said I was buying food items that I needed, and she wanted me to have what I needed. I never experienced anything like that. What character of God was revealed to me in this situation?

Then, there were times in my life when the devastation took my breath away. One of those times was the sudden death of my 23-year-old daughter. Her death was a time when I knew, deep down in my soul, that God was working on my behalf. It was a time when I felt as though someone or something else had to take over. I could have stopped functioning if I had not accepted medical attention and prescribed medication. I had prayer warriors who were unafraid to do what God said to do, literally covering me in prayer, standing in the gap at my home for an entire week, and encouraging me through that season of grief.

I know what God promised He would do in each situation. I watched Him work throughout very long seasons of warfare. But I still couldn't help being overwhelmed. I felt as though I was falling off a cliff. I tried to stand, but I was falling. At a routine well-check doctor's visit, I expressed these feelings, and we devised a plan to combat this bout of depression with medication. I took the pills for 30 days. I told God that I believed that was a temporary solution.

My routine doctor's appointment with my specialist was the next week. I talked to him about the situation as well. I told him about the prescribed medication, and as we ended our conversation, he looked at me and said, "May I pray for you?"

"What? Pray for me?" I had visited this doctor twice a year for more than twenty years. Our conversation was always about my health, nothing more.

He prayed scripture; he reminded God of His promises; he prophesied for a good five minutes. Talk about being blown away. I couldn't talk when I left the office. I sat in my car and cried. God showed up with the improbable. The Lord works through people and medication; we must recognize Him when He sends rescue. He is in control of our entire being. Our mental health is as important as our physical health.

Understanding the Names of God allows us to recognize Him more readily in everyday situations and circumstances. The names of God give us the feeling of being watched over, enabling us to prepare and endure the "Evil days."

As my Pastor explains, the evil days are "a particular season of intense spiritual engagement." As I look back over my life, I remember the evil days: as a house fire, the deaths of two spouses and a child, and a sibling living with an incurable disease. All my good days intertwined among those seasons, meant I had many more days of love, laughter, friendship, and abundant life than evil days.

The seventh day, a day that has everything God desires for us to have to do His will is available to us. The names and characteristics of God reveal what God expects from us and what we can expect from Him.

We can expect Elohim, our God, to be alive in our lives.

We can expect Adonai, our God to be Master—of us, and our circumstances.

We can expect El Shaddai, our God, to be mighty and perform miracles.

We can expect Yahweh, our God, to have a sacred relationship with us.

We can expect Yahweh Yireh, our God, to provide for us.

We are in covenant with a living God who always fulfills His promises. My prayer is that you will be able to recognize and acknowledge Him as you encounter Him in His many characteristics in your everyday life.

God continues to reveal Himself as we continually learn, understand, and live in the seventh day. Experiencing God as Yahweh, the covenant God, who is all-sufficient, we can know that He always will fulfill His promises. Our willingness to be a bond slave, devoted worshiper, and obedient reader-and-doer of the Word will allow us access to the provisions He has prepared for the seventh day. The seventh day is set apart, blessed, and sanctified.

PART I

Elohim

"The Living God"

CHAPTER ONE

Our God is Alive and All-Powerful

God is omnipotent, which means He can do anything. Elohim has the power and nature that can make anything possible. Being able is not synonymous with being willing. God is intentional about what conforms to His sovereign plan. When do we realize God can do anything but is not always willing to do everything? I believe it is when we acknowledge and accept His will for our everyday lives.

He has made us promises, and He will always keep His promises. He answers prayers, always. The Lord is able and willing to answer prayers that conform to His will, that transforms lives into the likeness of Him, and that will fulfill every promise He has made.

Elohim created the heavens and the earth; surely, He answers prayers. Of course, we all have had disappointment in our lives when our request does not manifest the way we envision the answer. Our faith can be shaken because we haven't prepared for a different outcome. It's not because we are not spiritual enough or that we don't have as much faith as we should. I have known many prayer warriors and intercessors, women, and men of God who feverishly bring prayer requests before God, and they receive an answer other than what they desired.

I believe God has the power to give us anything we want, but when He doesn't, we say God didn't answer our prayer. So why does He turn down requests that seem reasonable to us and appear to be a good thing?

My uncle Keith, a saved and sanctified saint of God, had been diagnosed with a debilitating disease. Everyone we knew began to pray for his healing. His healing would be a good thing. I would think this would be God's will. He wants us to be healthy, alive, and well.

What we didn't realize is that his diagnosis is what caused Keith Jr. to think about eternal life. Keith Jr. was brought to his father's funeral in handcuffs from the county jail. It was his father's death that drew him to accept Christ as his Savior that very day, which turned his life around. God surely was able to heal my uncle, but He intended to save the soul of my cousin. My cousin, Keith Jr., died a few years later of complications of diabetes.

My friend, Rosemary, had been praying about retiring from her job of 30 years. Her strategy was to go after one more promotion that would enable her to have a higher pay grade when she left the job market. A higher rate of pay would allow her to pay off their home loan and work fulltime at their Christian Couples Counseling Ministry with her husband, who had already departed his 9-to-5 job.

Rosemary did everything needed to enhance her expertise and was more than qualified for the promotion. She would be fulfilling what she believed to be God's will. What she did not realize was that her co-worker, who she had daily talks with about God's redemptive power in her marriage, was barely holding on by a thread to her marriage.

As prepared and qualified as Rosemary was for the promotion, someone else was selected. She was unable to retire that year, but the co-worker and her husband realized that they needed Jesus in their marriage. They submitted to counseling with Rosemary and her husband for the next year to make their marriage work. Rosemary was promoted to a much better position the following year.

As she began to work fulltime in her Christian Couples Counseling Ministry, her co-worker and her husband became servant leaders in the ministry, and their testimony has brought many couples to seek Godly counsel.

The answers to our prayers, in many instances, are answered differently than we desire because God wants to use our lives to impact the eternal life of others. We should be thankful that He doesn't always say "Yes" to our desires. He loves us too much to let us have an ordinary life when an extraordinary experience is possible. Elohim is all-powerful and can do anything.

CHAPTER TWO

It Had to Start Somewhere

Mary was my sister; her name was appropriate because she was a willing vessel, who allowed God to use her. She was the daughter raised in South Carolina by my grandaunt when my mother was sent to New York City to finish high school after giving birth.

My mother met and married my father a few years after high school, and I was born. I was an only child for their eight-year marriage. I traveled each year to South Carolina for two weeks of my summer vacation, beginning at age five.

Growing up, I didn't have a sense of Mary being my sister. To me, she was more like one of my ten cousins. It wasn't until Mary graduated from high school and moved to New York City with her best friend and one of my cousins, that we began to bond as sisters. She was a loving and kind-hearted person.

Hanging out at their apartment was newfound freedom for me. My weekends were curfew free.

I introduced her to her first husband. He was my supervisor at Bronx State (Psychiatric) Hospital, where I worked as a recreational student aide while in high school. They had a beautiful wedding. Mary could cook and sew and enjoyed doing all the delightful homemaker things. During their marriage, Mary discovered that she would be unable to have children. She also found out that she had sarcoidosis, a debilitating disease that would eventually affect her vital organs.

After six years of quietly putting up with her husband's indiscretions, Mary asked for a divorce, packed her bags, and moved to Atlanta, Georgia. She didn't know anyone in Atlanta, but she would make it her home. I admired her for not letting fear of the unknown deter her. She had a plan to escape. Mild-mannered Mary had a bank account, an apartment, and a job with a major corporation in Atlanta before moving. Her husband, if nothing else, was an excellent provider. Mary did not have to pay household bills and was able to save money from her paycheck, so she relocated seamlessly.

Meanwhile, back in New York City, I had given birth to my second daughter, Amira. My marriage was very shaky. The day before Easter, after making up with my husband for the umpteenth time, I left home with my daughters to spend the night with my mother. We would go to the Easter Mass with her the next day. I remember turning around and going back to the apartment because I had forgotten something. I got a chance to tell my husband good-bye once again and reminded him to buy the girls an Easter basket and to bring it to my mother's house the next day when he came up for dinner. Despite everything we'd been through, Derrick loved and cared so much for his daughters. Helema was his #1 D.J. and Amira, the apple of his eye.

At mass on Easter Sunday morning, 1980, a bizarre feeling came over me. By this time in my life, I knew about God and knew he was there. With all the "religious instructions" that I had taken in the Catholic Church, having received Holy Communion and Confirmation, I had a shallow relationship with God. It was always about me. I prayed when I needed something.

This Sunday, an uncontrollable desire to pray swept over my total being. There was a desperate prayer in my heart. I needed the Lord to help me get through something, not knowing what it would be. I had a feeling that something was about to happen, and my strength would not be enough. I was always in control, so this feeling was strange to me.

It wasn't until after Easter dinner that I learned why.

I began to get angry with my husband because, once again, he let us down. He had not called or brought the girls their Easter baskets as he had promised he would.

As we were clearing the dinner dishes, the phone rang at my mother's apartment. It was the New York City Police Department trying to contact me. My husband managed to stay out of jail during our five years of marriage, but right away, I knew that he had gotten in some kind of trouble.

My mind flashed back to his promise to me the day we had gone to get our marriage license. That was the day I found out that his last name, the name that I knew him by and thought would be mine, wasn't his. He explained that because he had committed a felony under his real name, he had begun to use his mother's maiden name as his last name. A red flag went up, but I pretended not to see it.

I then sat down and demanded that he tell me everything about his life. The story of his family ties to gangsters in Harlem, burglaries in China Town, running numbers, and drug deals was scary but exciting. He had been in and out of juvenile detention centers, jail, or prison most of his life since his youth. He was 32, ten years older than me. I was confident that I could change him, and I was determined to do so. I could love him enough to make him turn his life around.

He said he was tired of his old life. He wanted to start life over, with me at his side. I believed him, and I thought he could be a good husband and father. I would show him a different life. We would live happily ever after.

I married him using both last names, which would be very crucial for my daughters later in life.

As the years went by, I knew in my heart that it would only be a matter of time before something terrible would happen. My husband's attempt to appear reputable, by working a civil service job as an admissions clerk at a local hospital, was a way to keep me from harassing him about his criminal activity.

I went to the 47th precinct, which was within walking distance from my mother's apartment. A patrol car would meet me there to take me to the 52nd precinct, which was the precinct closest to our apartment in the South Bronx. New York City Transit was on strike at the time. Public transportation was at a standstill.

On my way to the precinct, I stopped at a corner bodega and bought a couple of packs of cigarettes. I figured it was the last thing that I would do for him. There wasn't going to be any visitations by me to the jail. I had had it. I had done all I was willing to do. I warned him that, eventually, his activities would lead him to prison or his grave. I paid a high price to learn that I could not change anyone or expect them to live up to my expectations, but I did have choices. I could choose to live and not merely exist, waiting for something to happen, afraid to be truly happy.

In the precinct, the mood was very somber. A detective came out to meet me. He told me that my brother-in-law, Mike, was also there, and he would be out to talk to me.

Mike came into the room. Mike was Derrick's youngest brother, who also lived in the Bronx, had already made phone calls to their brother, Chauncey, who lived in Atlanta, and his sister, Nanine, who had recently moved to Philly.

I was about to tell him all the things I was no longer willing to put up with, when he said very calmly, " Sit down."

As I sat down, a queasy feeling began to flood my stomach. The look on his face froze me in place. Then his words dropped like bombs "Someone killed Derrick. He was in the handball court at the park on 173rd St and Cortona Ave."

Cortona Park was not far from our apartment. It was a lively park, famous for its views, its trees, and its pond. From high points in the park, you could see the Palisades of New Jersey to the west and the towers of the Brooklyn Bridge to the South. The park had twenty tennis courts, twenty-six handball courts, nine playgrounds. There is where we went to listen to the new sounds of "Grand Master Flash and the Furious Five," who performed the rhymes of Rap music, fresh on the scene.

Mike told me, "The police think it was someone he knew because he was shot while sitting down, and this could indicate that he was comfortable with the person and was not expecting what happened. Derrick was shot in the head. The bullet went through his hand. He must have put his hand up to shield his head."

This news made me feel as though something hit me in the chest and then in the stomach. My heart hurt, and then my stomach began to ache. I could not speak for a few seconds. So many things were running through my mind. After a few minutes, I remember calling my mother and telling her what happened. I don't know what I was feeling: I had to be sure she would take good care of my girls.

Mike had already identified the body.

With that done, I took a cab back to my mother's apartment.

10

CHAPTER THREE

The Village Awaits

O n holidays, my childhood friends who grew up in the same housing project building would come home to their parents' apartments for dinner, where we would catch up with one another. It was Easter Sunday, and all of my childhood friends were waiting at my mother's apartment when I arrived back there. The answer to everything in those days was, "Give her a good stiff drink."

So I drank. No one knew what to say because it had never happened to anyone we knew. I had never been to a funeral. I had one friend who died when we were sixteen. That was the only time I even thought about death. We lived in a fairytale, Cinderella world. Death, divorce, homosexuality, or drug abuse, was never discussed with us by our parents.

Once everyone went home, and the girls were in bed, I sat in the middle of my mother's bedroom floor. Mom stared at me but did not say a word. Not even my mother could fathom this situation. There was no advice or words of wisdom she could offer me at that moment.

My devastation turned to anger. I wanted to know why and how something like this could happen. Though my brother and I grew up raised in New York City Housing, we never experienced what I thought of as poverty. I didn't know that we were considered low income. Our story is so different from the negative stories we hear about life growing up in the projects. Welfare was not a way of life for most of the families that we knew.

Our apartment's living room was furnished with a white six-foot Castro convertible sofa, red wall-to-wall carpet, coffee and end tables from Bassett, and beautiful drapes. Both my mother and father had jobs, as did all of my friends' parents. Most of my friends lived in two-parent households. My father was a butcher and my mother a secretary. My mother always prepared breakfast and dinner. My brother and I were never hungry. We had the clothes that we needed, took music and dance lessons, belonged to Scout troops and received an allowance each week if we did our chores and got good grades. Where we lived, in the Northeast Bronx, was a newly developed area.

We were one of the first families to move into Edenwald Public Housing. Everything was brand new. There were dairies and wooded park areas for Saturday afternoon picnics. Being very close to Mt. Vernon, New York, the schools were predominately white. I was actually the only black child in my kindergarten class, where I was bussed to school because of the landmark decision of Brown v. Board of Education, four years earlier.

I can honestly say that I did not think there was anything different about me from my classmates. My mother still tells the story of how I came home from school with my class picture and challenged her to find me in the photo. I don't think I ever got over the hurt I felt when she busted out in laughter.

The building where we lived was home for families that would allow us to know and learn about many cultures. We lived on the 9th floor of a building that was 14 stories high, with 10 apartments on each floor. On our floor alone lived an elderly Jewish couple, the Habers, who were Holocaust survivors and taught me the difference between Yiddish and Hebrew; an Italian family, Angie, Joey, and their kids; Marie Castellano, who would become my Godmother at my Catholic Confirmation; a West Indian family from Barbados; the Scotts, whose dad owned the neighborhood barbershop and whose mother was a nurse; the Melendez family from Puerto Rico with their two sons; The Heygoods, from Charleston South Carolina, where the father was a postal worker and the mother was a stay-at-home mom who was there to receive me, along with her three kids, home from school in the afternoons.

There were the Neelys: Mack, an EMT, Brenda, a nurse, and their two daughters; Mrs. Logan, who was the building hairdresser and her daughter; the Johns, who worked for the telephone company, had one daughter; the Merrett's were Shinnecock Indian, and the dad was a dental student who afforded some of us the opportunity to visit the reservation where their relatives lived for the annual Labor Day Pow-Wow. At that time, we were not even aware that the Shinnecock reservation was in Southampton, Long Island, where today only the rich and famous can afford to live.

The Lowerys, the Beacons, the Matthews, the Nichols, the Stevens, the Batts, the Rosados, the Saunders, and the Carrols all made up the village that raised the children of this project building. We grew-up the way my parents thought the American dream was supposed to play out: We believed that we could be or accomplish whatever we desired. The sky was the limit. There was never a discussion about divorce, death, or anything negative—with the exception of sex outside of marriage and the consequences. Only two out of maybe twenty of the girls I knew personally actually became teen moms.

CHAPTER FOUR

The Cinderella Dream Died

The days of preparation for the funeral and the funeral service were all a blur. I was glad that it was over. Now was the time I needed to figure out what to do next. I was angry because I was unprepared for this experience of "death." I would later find out that I was not prepared for a lot of things. I would then experience things I could not even imagine. I was not in control. I needed to be in control of everything that happened to me, so this was troubling.

At the time of Derrick's death, my family lived in an apartment building that had a doorman and security in the lobby. The hallways had carpet, and the apartments had parquet floors. We even had an apartment-sized washer and dryer hidden in one of the walk-in closets. Our bedroom had a window unit air conditioner. I thought we were living large. I looked up to the heavens as I stood on the cement balcony of my apartment, which had a view of the South Bronx and all its abandoned tenement buildings. I told God I knew there had to be more to this life. I needed something more; I needed a change in my life. I let God know that if He showed me what to do, I would do it.

My mother was in Atlanta visiting my sister Mary. She took my eldest daughter, Helema, who was four. They had only been there for three days, and she fell in love with Georgia. My mother was born in Savannah, Georgia, but was raised in a small town in South Carolina, a short distance from Hilton Head Island. Mom had not been back for decades. The South had changed. She was adamant about me coming to visit right away. I could not imagine living anywhere else but in New York City. I had visited other places but did not consider living anywhere else.

I was still on childcare leave from my New York City job as a 911 operator. I decided to go to Atlanta as my last hurrah before seriously considering accepting a position as a Legal Assistant for the Queens District Attorney's Office. The DA's office was not really where I wanted to work, it would be at least a 2-hour subway ride each way, each day, from my apartment in the Bronx, but I didn't want to go back to my last assignment, either. I had attended John Jay College of Criminal Justice and worked as a Correctional Counselor while attending school. Having worked at Rikers Island and The Toombs, my pie-in-the-sky idea of becoming an attorney dissolved. The passion was gone. I had decided that criminal law was no longer going to be my focus. I turned my attention to business administration not understanding why.

I knew God heard my prayers, but I did not understand the covenant I had with Him or His will for my life. I believe that on Easter Sunday while sitting in the church, when I asked God to help me, and again on my balcony when I asked Him to show me something different from the life I was living, He already had everything worked out for me. I simply did not understand my journey and destiny.

One thing I do know is that He chooses us—we don't choose Him. Yes, we have a choice in accepting and walking in salvation, but He loves us first. Once we become aware of Him in our everyday life, something changes. Being sensitive to the Spirit takes time and willingness and obedience to His will.

"3 C's of Life: Choices, Chances, Changes
You must make a choice, to take a chance,
or your life will never change."
-Zig Ziglar

CHAPTER FIVE

Change is Gonna Come

I booked a flight for me and my baby girl, Amira, who was 14-months old, to fly to Atlanta, Georgia. I believe it was the best thing that could have happened in my life at this time. From the very start, I was in awe of Atlanta. The airport was new, vibrant, and exciting. When I stepped off the plane, there were two great looking guys waiting to meet me. Mary had sent her friend and his brother to pick me up. What a wonderful welcome. Both of these guys were extremely easy on the eyes.

We rode to Decatur, Georgia, a suburb of Atlanta, where Mary lived. During this time, "Spanish Trace Apartments" was the most popular place to live in South DeKalb County.

Driving down I-20 and seeing the beautiful trees along the highway was wonderful. When we turned into the entrance of the complex, I was ecstatic. We passed what I would find

17

out later was the clubhouse. I thought they couldn't possibly live here. I couldn't hold it in. I had to ask "You live here? You really live here?"

Summer was in full bloom. I saw men and women in swimsuits around a beautiful swimming pool, diving and swimming and having a great time. Who would have thought that I could come home to this kind of atmosphere?

When Mary opened the apartment door and the cool air hit me, I wondered how many window units it took to make it feel cool all over the apartment. There was wall to wall carpet, a dishwasher, and garbage disposal. I had never seen a dishwasher or garbage disposal personally or knew anyone who had central air conditioning. When Mary told me how much she paid for rent, I knew this apartment complex would be my new home. She was paying a third of what I paid for rent in New York.

As weeks past and Mom went back home to New York, Mary and I began to bond. I rented a townhouse apartment right next to Mary's. I flew back to the Bronx to pack a few things that I wanted to take with me, hired a moving van to move the few items needed, and I gave my mother instructions to give away everything else. I was back on the plane, bound for Atlanta and my new home, that same weekend.

CHAPTER SIX

I Just Didn't Know

Finding a church was as hard as finding a job. Each Sunday, I would attend a service at a different neighborhood Catholic Church and each Sunday, I would come home disappointed. I was not inspired. I was expecting something new.

I kept reminding myself of the night I prayed on my balcony in the Bronx. I was going to wait for His promise. He was going to show me new things, and He had never let me down. Elohim always keeps His promises.

Mary finally convinced me to go with her to her church. I had been putting it off after she told me she attended a Pentecostal Holiness church. I had never heard of the Pentecostal denomination, Church of God in Christ (COGIC). All I knew was that holiness women where I came from wore long skirts and wrapped up their hair or wore one of those doilies on their heads. That was not for me. Mary promised me that it would not be like I had envisioned it. She was right.

Immediately, I knew that God was guiding me. I was at the end of my rope. I had not found a job, and my money was low. When the Pastor called for salvation, I couldn't stay seated. I knew God was with me, but this Jesus being in my heart was something new, and I wanted Jesus. As I walked to the front of the church and the people began to clap and shout, I wanted to run, to hurry and get what was waiting for me.

There was newfound freedom in understanding the sufficiency of Christ's sacrifice on the cross. I wanted to be a part of the body of Christ, where salvation is a gift from God. I would learn and understand that I could not earn salvation. Performing works of penance, praying to the Saints, or any other human-made ritual would not bring me to salvation or increase the amount of grace needed to fulfill the will of God. I merely had to have faith and trust in Jesus Christ alone for the forgiveness of my sins.

The pastor asked for a sacrificial offering. I didn't know what a sacrificial offering meant, but I had $1.75. I put it in the offering basket, not even sure if I had enough gas to drive home. I believed that everything was going to be okay.

It was that night I decided I had to do what it took to make a living for my family. I had watched my father go fishing on the weekends after working all week as a butcher for Oscar Mayer, come home, and sell fresh fish out of the back of his station wagon. He did what it took. Any job that was available and offered to me, I was going to accept.

The next day as I was driving through a shopping plaza, I noticed a sign that said, "Cashier Wanted." At this point, any job was better than nothing. I had been searching for work for weeks with the idea that I had to get paid at least what I received in New York. My husband's life insurance funds had begun to dwindle, and social security for the girls was very little. My husband had not worked on legitimate jobs very much in his lifetime. I had to file for social security under both his last names so that they could combine the incomes so that the girls would be eligible for benefits. It was a good thing that I had married him under both last names and that

I insisted that he work a 9-to-5 job the five years we were married.

Here is where the experience with Elohim becomes real. I realized that when I am weak, He is strong. He will keep His promises. He always answers prayer. When we access resources that we need, we are in His will. His plan for us most times will not look like what we envisioned. He will give us power and strength. God can provide us with a position that we're are not even qualified for so that He would be the only one to get the glory.

I applied for the cashier's position and handed the District Manager my resume. The job was at a new gas station. I knew nothing about the gasoline business. I had just recently learned to drive and bought my first car from an auction.

After reviewing my resume and an extensive interview, the District Manager offered me a position, not as a cashier but as a manager. I had never managed anything before. I had never hired or fired anyone. I had never prepared a payroll or inventory. I became the manager of one of the first self-service gas stations in Atlanta. I knew it had to be God. It would be His grace that allowed me to acquire a job that I had no previous experience in doing and receive a salary that would sustain my household. The business courses I took in college helped me develop my skills in sales, marketing, and promotion. These skills would be the key to my successful career in the future.

I wanted a change and something different, and I got it. I had sincere trust in God.

I would remain in that C.O.G.I.C ministry for ten years. When God said it was time to leave that ministry, it was very hard. My sister and friends all went to that church. They couldn't understand why I wanted to leave. My girls insisted that I attend a church in my neighborhood with them because they wanted to sing in the Youth for Christ Choir. Our church did not have a youth choir, only a children's' choir.

To be honest, the first Sunday I attended this new church, I was not impressed with the service. It was, as I came to understand, a "traditional Baptist church," which was a little different, a little more subdued. The congregation was not very big at this time, but it was growing. The pastor was new, and the church was building a larger sanctuary to accommodate the growth.

What I was impressed with was the focus that was placed on the youth. The Pastor at the time was young, unmarried, and conveyed a passion and care for our youth. I would become a part of this ministry that began to grow in leaps and bounds. This was a progressive ministry that would be instrumental in my step from "attending church" to a supernatural encounter and a relationship with the true and living God.

CHAPTER SEVEN

If God Doesn't Heal, It's Not Because He Can't

It had been ten years since Mary had heart surgery. Her illness, sarcoidosis, had begun to take its toll and affect her vital organs. I recall the day I walked into her room in ICU at Emory University Hospital when Mary was the seventh recipient and the first female to receive a defibrillator implanted in her chest. I remember trying to prepare myself for her to die. There were so many wires and tubes running into her body. Her body was cold and hard.

Mary described an out of body experience after her surgery. She felt as though she was floating above her body, watching them operate on her. As her body stood at the gates of heaven, her instructions were to go back. Her purpose and destiny were not complete. Three little girls needed her.

God answered our prayers, and she was able to walk out of that hospital. Mary began an intense quest to serve God even more. She did things that we, as a family, did not always understand. Mary became a guardian for Tanya, a ten-day-old baby girl, only one month after having major surgery. She didn't have the strength even to carry her.

Mary received disability from her job at Coca Cola, but she fought her way to volunteer at church and became a viable part of the office staff and in charge of the food bank. She made sure that any family in need had food. She always had a room in her home for those who needed a temporary place to live.

Mary prepared meals as though she were a chef and cooked countless Sunday dinners for all our friends and family to come and fellowship after church on Sundays. There was no one I knew who disliked her. Mary helped me raise my two daughters. They loved her with all their hearts.

We watched Mary grow weaker and weaker, but she would not give up. Her eyesight began to fail. She would fall asleep each time she sat still for more than a few minutes. A valve in her heart was leaking. There was nothing the doctors could do to repair it. She was not a candidate for a heart transplant because the disease would cause a new heart also to deteriorate. On the night of June 26, 1998, we talked and talked. She said to me, "If I could get up out of this bed, I would never sit down on God again because He gave me a new heart. Don't you sit down on God."

I didn't get it. As far as I was concerned, Mary was always on point with God. A few days later, she died. My sister had so much faith. She believed that God had given her a new heart. Indeed He had given her a new heart, a heart for Him.

At the time, I could not understand why she had to leave us. Not prepared for her to go, I believed God would perform a miracle. I had prayed for God to heal her and once again let her walk out of that hospital. He had done it before; He could do it again. Did I not have enough faith? Why did this happen?

When I went to Mary's house from the hospital that day, I walked into her bedroom. On her bed was her Bible opened to the last thing she read before going to the hospital. It was a comfort to me as I read John 17:4-5, *I have glorified You on the earth. I have finished the work which You have given Me to do. And now, O Father, glorify Me together with Yourself, with the glory which I had with You before the world was (NKJV).*

I then understood. Mary completed what she was supposed to do, but she loved the Lord so much that she wanted to do even more than her reasonable service for God. I was experiencing Elohim as the All-Powerful God who used Mary's life to impact the eternal well-being of my life, the lives of my daughters, her daughter, and just about everyone with whom she came in contact. So the answer to our prayer was what was best for us. All the faith in the world is not enough to keep a person alive if it's not in God's perfect will. It is predestined that we transform into the image of Christ, and that won't happen until we see Him face to face.

"Don't sit down on God," stayed in my mind. By watching Mary minister to people, I understood that I had to be a participant in God's will for my life. With this, comes the understanding that Elohim, the "Us" who created the heavens and the earth, has given us an impossible task of obeying His commands. Once we recognize our weakness and that we can't do anything without Him, He will send His Spirit to give us the power to obey His commands.

There is no sense in wasting time trying to do it in our own strength. Nothing is impossible with God. I won't sit down on Elohim, the God that answers prayers, keeps His promises, and transforms lives.

During the ten years before Mary died, I married my high school sweetheart. The Bible says, "A man shall find a wife after his own heart." Dorian heard that my first husband, Derrick, had died. He went to my mother's apartment in New York and left a letter for her to forward to me. When I received the letter, I was romantically involved with someone else, so I did not respond to his message.

Months past, and, during a routine cleaning out of a junk drawer, I came across the letter again. Since my previous relationship had ended, I figured I would give Dorian a call. He was ecstatic to hear from me. It had been sixteen years since we had seen each other. He made immediate arrangements to come to Georgia to see me.

Dorian arrived prepared to stay for the weekend but stayed for a week. We caught up on everything that happened to us in the past sixteen years. Dorian worked for the New York Transit Authority, and his job was waiting for him to return. He promised to come back to Atlanta for his birthday the following month.

We talked for hours every day by telephone. We reminisced about our high school days and the dances he took me to at Crawford Memorial United Methodist Church and summers at his parent's summer home on Martha's Vineyard. We talked about the last time we saw each other at the "Bridgefield Civic League's Debutante Ball." It was the first time that the "project girls" were invited to participate in the cotillion.

Weeks before the cotillion, Dorian and I had a huge argument. I had to find another escort for my big evening of being "Introduced to Society." I was grateful that my friend, Larry, was willing to escort me at such short notice. I did not see Dorian again until the night of the cotillion. We locked eyes. It was as though we had never been apart. I wanted to tell him I was sorry. It was as though there was no one else in the room until we were interrupted by his date.

When I realized he had escorted another girl to my cotillion, I was furious. I let him have it. I turned to her and reprimanded her for daring to interrupt the conversation Dorian and I was having. We were one of the most well-known couples. We had been dating since junior high school. She had to know Dorian was on the rebound. That was the last time I saw him or her. I was sixteen.

As Dorian's birthday approached, we began talking about marriage. When it was time for him to return to Atlanta, we each had taken a blood test, me in Atlanta, and he in New York. He arrived on his birthday with a wedding ring. We went to get our marriage license that day and arranged to marry the very next day.

I had two concerns about this marriage: The first concern was the sermon my Pastor had ministered about Christians not marrying in civil proceedings. I knew in my spirit that it was right to marry him, but my Pastor's words stayed in my mind, and the civil ceremony we had arranged troubled me.

When we arrived at the courthouse, we could not find the judge that was supposed to perform the ceremony. I began to pray, "What now, Lord?" I looked up at the directory once again to see if I could locate the judge, but what I saw was "Chaplain."

We went to his office, and when he opened his office door, he said, "You want a Christian wedding, don't you?" I believe God made the arrangements for this union. If you have the desire to please God and let Him be in control, He will direct your path.

The second issue was whether or not Dorian and I were unequally yoked. The sermon preached on this subject concerned me. What does it mean to be "unequally yoked"? Would I be out of order to marry this man? God gave me peace about this, even though I didn't have a full understanding of the scripture. I knew it was better to marry than to possibly slip into sinful practices. I had to be an example for my girls.

Dorian believed in God and didn't have a problem with going to church. As young kids, we attended the same church where he received baptism, and his father was a deacon. I was going to believe that God would not fail me; He never did.

I began to study the scripture about being unequally yoked. Revealed to me was that Paul's letter in 2 Corinthians 6:14 was not encouraging isolation from unbelievers but was discouraging compromise or aligning themselves with their sinful values and practices. God was urging us to maintain our integrity and avoid anything that might influence or undermine us from following Christ. This warning would also include people who advocate false teaching or mixing the worship of Christ with other idols.

We do business every day with unbelievers, but it would be unwise to go into business with an unbeliever. This scripture could relate to dating and marriage, but 1 Corinthians 7:14 speaks specifically to marriage. *"For the unbelieving husband is sanctified by the wife, and the unbelieving wife is sanctified by the husband; otherwise, your children would be unclean, but now they are holy" (NKJV).*

W. E. Vine, an English scholar, and theologian observed that "The unbelieving husband or wife is relatively set apart through his or her believing partner. And abiding in the natural union, instead of breaking it by leaving, receives a spiritual influence holding the possibility of actual conversion."

The first Sunday, we attended church together as a married couple, the Lord touched Dorian's heart, and he re-dedicated his life to Christ.

A couple of years into our marriage, Dorian's son, Donald, from his first marriage, came to live with us. (Dorian married the girl he brought to the cotillion). With his son and my two daughters, we had a ready-made family. Our marriage, with a blended family, was challenging at times, yet Dorian still wanted a child of our own. I thought Donald coming to live with us would curtail my husband's desire to have a baby, but it didn't.

CHAPTER EIGHT

I Was in Control of My Life

Let me back up: After Derrick died, I had decided that if I had not remarried by the time I was 30-years old, I was going to have a tubal ligation. When my 30th birthday came and went, I decided to wait one more year, believing God for another husband. By age 31, I gave up. I still thought that God would send me another husband, but a baby was going to be out of the picture. I was getting too old to have children, and I needed to take control and get on with my career. I had a tubal ligation performed in April; Dorian and I married in August of the same year.

One morning shortly after Dorian's son, Donald, came to live with us, almost three years into our marriage, I walked into our bathroom and realized that my monthly women's supply was untouched. I went to my calendar, and I was five days late. No, no, this could not be happening. I had decided that I did not want to be pregnant ever again. Being pregnant was a challenge for me. I was sick most of the nine months.

Dorian kept talking about me having another baby. Was I glad I had my tubes tied? Yes, I was. Dorian spoke to my doctor about reversing the tubal ligation surgery. He wanted a baby. I was secretly glad that I could not get pregnant. I was standing in my bedroom wondering why the box in the bathroom was still full.

I went to the women's clinic to have a pregnancy test. After two urine tests and then a blood test, I accepted my pregnancy. I was furious. I called my doctor's office and demanded that he explain how this could happen.

At this time, I was the producer of FemCare, female healthcare, cable TV talk show. I invited my doctor, who had performed the tubal ligation, to be a guest on the show to tell America how this could have happened to me. Yes, tubal ligations are indeed only 99 percent effective. Well, at least that is what I thought when I believed I was in control of my life. I happened to be in that one percent that would get pregnant.

After a couple of weeks of getting used to the idea of being pregnant—and over the morning sickness—I began to get excited. Dorian was so happy; I guess it spilled over to make me glad to give him the child he wanted.

At a Wednesday night Bible study, I was standing up, praising God, and a sharp pain hit me. I went to the restroom and was horrified to see blood running down my legs. On the way to the emergency room, I began to pray that everything would be okay. I had a miscarriage, something I would have never thought could happen.

My devastation caused me to cry continuously for a week. I talked to God passionately about this. I needed to know why this was happening. It was so perplexing because, two months before, I was angry about the fact that I was pregnant.

I believe, for me, that God was showing me that I was not in charge of me. He was. He introduced Himself to me as Adonai; I began slowly to turn over control of my life to Him.

Giving over control of your life is not easy. I would present God a situation for Him to handle and then take it back and try to fix it myself. After messing it up again, I would give it back to Him. I had to relinquish control. He was in control of everything. I must accept His answers because He only wants the best for me.

Six months later, tubal ligation still in place; I was pregnant again. This time I was grateful. It was a very complicated pregnancy, but I made it through and delivered a healthy baby boy. We named Raheem.

PART II

Adonai

"Lord, Master, or Owner"

CHAPTER NINE

Our God is Lord and Master

Adonai is God as Lord and Master. The true meaning of the name Adonai is "master or owner." We must understand God's outright ownership of all things in Heaven and Earth. If we claim God is our Lord and Master, then our role must be that of a bond-slave to Adonai. Some people have a problem with the word slave because of the adverse connotation associated with it, but we must become more than servants. The nature of a servant is servitude, free to work for any master. A slave, purchased for a price, has an owner or master. The essence of a slave is obedience. After a debt is paid, a bond-slave by choice elects to continue to serve that master.

We are not our own because we have been "bought with a price." The precious blood of Jesus paid a debt for us. We must choose to serve our Master with obedience.

Adonai has the right to expect us to obey His commandants, whether it is complicated or straightforward, fashionable, or unpopular. There will be a time when we need to take action on things that don't make sense to us or to wait, for no apparent reason, for something God promised. We tend to take the situation out of God's hands to do it ourselves. It never works out.

When it doesn't work out, He is willing and able to correct the situations to enable His will to be carried out. He is trying to teach us to live by faith in Him, not by our motive. His desire is for us to submit to His will because we trust Him. Our obedience should be motivated by genuine respect for Him as the Master.

The world system teaches us to believe that we are in control of our destiny. Not true. The Lord is not dependent on anyone or anything, but we are dependent on Him for everything. Our education may trick us into believing that we can handle everything that life brings our way in our strength, which keeps God from moving on our behalf.

It is God who calls us to service. Our "reasonable service" (Romans 12:1) is to present our body as a living sacrifice, yielding entirely to the will of our Master so that His desires become our desires. He seeks our higher good.

Many of us resist the idea of God having complete control over our lives, but whether we know Him as Master or not, He is the Master. We can't make Him Master; He already is Master of everything. Our relationship with Him is not one-sided. In return for yielding to God's will, we recognize that He is in our midst and, therefore, will manage our affairs when we are in service. He is the sustainer and will drive out our enemies. He will give direction in service with His loving guidance.

Adonai wants us to stop trying to control our destiny. It is the only way we can begin to enter into the fullness of the Lord and access His power needed to fulfill our destiny.

CHAPTER TEN

So, You Think You're In Control?

I remember standing in my kitchen preparing dinner one evening, and I said, "Thank you, Lord, because I have it all." I was married to my high school sweetheart, we owned our own home, our children were healthy, and we had good jobs and went to church. Life was good. We had it going on.

Then it happened: Dorian hurt his back, and the doctor admitted him to the hospital. The doctors put him in traction and placed an IV in his hand to administer pain medications. After a couple of days, the IV became infected. The doctors tried everything to get the infection to go away. After switching antibiotics several times, they began to run all types of tests to determine what could be causing the infection.

I called his hospital room the day he was supposed to get the results of all the tests. He was not taking phone calls. I called his doctor, and she informed me that I would have to speak to him about the test results.

A little nervous and confused, I went to the hospital. Dorian's room was very dark. The light was off, and the drapes were drawn, even though it was 2:00 in the afternoon. I walked over to the bed, and I could see the tears slowly falling from his eyes. I asked what was wrong, but he kept saying over and over again that he could not tell me what the doctor had found. I tried to convince him that everything would be fine and that I would be there to help him through whatever it was.

He then told me that he tested positive for AIDS. I was horrified and could hardly catch my breath. How could this happen? How could this be? I sat down because I couldn't think. We did not fit the profile for this disease. We were not IV drug users or homosexuals, and I had no reason to believe that my husband had been unfaithful. We had been married for fifteen years. How could this have happened?

We sat there in the dark for what seemed like hours. Finally, I said, "You will get through this; I will be here for you." It never crossed my mind that I could be infected. I knew God would not let this happen to me, not me.

The next day, we met with Dorian's doctor. He asked us several questions, trying to understand how Dorian could have contracted the disease. Since we honestly denied any marital infidelity, he asked us if we had been in contact with anyone's blood.

I thought about it and said, "No." I was about to suggest that they do the test over because it had to be a mistake when Dorian remembered a fight some years before at the prison where he worked as a corrections officer. It was no small quarrel. It took many corrections officers to break up the blood bath.

My perfect life was now upside down. My stomach knotted up, and I felt nauseated. All I could think about was death. We now had to prepare to die.

During this time, most of the anti-viral drugs were experimental. My t-cells at that point were in the normal range, so I was not a candidate for medication. I was infuriated at the fact that I would have to wait until my t-cell count was under 400 before I would be prescribed medication. I could not believe that I would have to wait until this "virus" overtook my body and deteriorated my health before I could receive treatment.

I was not in control. That was the bottom line.

During this time, we also discovered that my 16-year-old daughter, Amira, was pregnant. Because of our close mother-daughter relationship, I knew within days. After a positive test result from the doctor, it was as though I lost all sensibility. I started talking crazy to my daughter. I began telling her things that were contrary to what I had come to believe and taught her.

I thank God that she grew up in the church—no, I thank God that she grew up with the Word of God. When I forgot who was justly in charge of our lives, Amira knew in her heart and reminded me of what I taught her and what God had promised. She realized her indiscretion, repented, and was genuinely sorry but was not going to compound her mistake. She understood that this would be her responsibility, and she was going to handle it.

CHAPTER ELEVEN

His Word Never Comes Back Void

Amira never stopped attending church service on Sunday and continued to go to school. She endured the loathsome stares of some people, as her stomach grew substantially. My heart ached for her. I wished I could ease her pain.

All of my friends and family were supportive. They showered her with encouragement and lots of parenting information. I praise God for two women, in particular, Kim and Pat. They let her know that people make mistakes, but God never makes mistakes.

No matter what it looks like, God is sovereign and is in control of every situation. Finally, I felt like we could get through this when her doctor called. She did not want to alarm us, but one of Amira's blood tests was abnormal. The test results revealed that the baby could be born with Down's

Syndrome. The doctor wanted her to come in to do an ultrasound and have an amniocentesis.

My family and friends, my mother and her prayer partners, began to pray. Truly, blessing came down. Amira and I talked about this challenge and prayed. We knew that, if this was to be, then the Lord would once again give us the strength to deal with it. We had to turn it over to Him. This was something I could not take back from God's control. It seemed as though I was being placed in situations that made it perfectly clear that I was not in control of anything.

Amira gave birth to Micah, a perfect baby boy. Micah's father, Cameron, stepped up to the plate and cut the umbilical cord when his son entered into this world. It was a blessing to see this 17-year old beginning to make the transition from boy to man and father. Amira began working part-time and graduated from high school.

My first grandson made us a family of four living generations. Four generations on both sides of Micah's family attended his baby dedication. His mother, father, grandmothers, grandfathers, and great-grandmothers shared in the celebration of dedicating this child back to the Lord, for he was truly another gift from God. I was no longer a reluctant grandmother. It was a reality that God never makes mistakes, and He is always in control.

CHAPTER TWELVE

It's Really Not About You

In the following months, when self-pity would set in, the Lord would show me that when things happen it is not necessarily about me. It is all about Him and the Kingdom of God and Him being glorified.

The phone was ringing, but I could not move. I slowly awoke from a deep sleep. I was so weak. I had worked all week at the "Spirit and Truth" conference. I remember thinking, "I must be exhausted." It took all my strength to reach the phone. I then realized something was wrong. I had no strength.

I got the phone up to my ear. It was my girlfriend, Denise. She immediately became alarmed. "What's the matter?" she asked.

"I don't know. Call back and let the phone ring until Amira answers; tell her to come upstairs, I am so sick."

I barely got the phone back in its cradle when it began to ring again. It seemed like it rang a hundred times. I didn't have the strength to call downstairs to Amira to let her know I was in trouble. She finally answered the phone and came upstairs to find me shivering as though I were in the North Pole. I was wrapped in three blankets. She helped me to the bathroom where I got fully dressed. I figured it would help keep me warm.

As soon as I finished getting dressed, I broke out into a sweat. All of a sudden, I was burning up. I had to throw off all the blankets. A few minutes later I was shivering again. I was waiting for my doctors' office to open at 9:00, sharp. Amira was calling to see if I could be seen right away; at 9:05 a.m., we were in the car headed to the doctor's office in Atlanta.

Once we arrived, they administered the usual battery of blood tests. It was not long before the doctor told me that my blood did show signs of some type of bacteria. He immediately wanted to admit me to the hospital. I really did not want to stay. I was too concerned about my family to stay away. The doctor then told me the alternative would be to stay there at the office and let them administer antibiotics intravenously.

After five hours of drug intake, I was given a prescription for more antibiotics to take over the weekend. I was to report back on Monday morning first thing. I stayed in bed all weekend. On Sunday evening, my doctor called and told me that something was growing in my blood, but they had not identified it at that time. He reiterated that I needed to come to the office first thing Monday morning.

Upon my arrival Monday morning, I was escorted right back to the IV room and given more antibiotics. When my doctor arrived, he came right in to see me. He told me that what I had was E-coli poisoning. He told me that if I had not come to the office when I did, I would have been dead. This really unnerved me. In my quiet time, lying there with the IV in my arm, the Spirit of the Lord began to minister to me.

The Lord was showing me that He was in control of everything. I needed to relinquish my total being to Him. HIV was not a death sentence, but a life sentence of serving Him. He showed me that if He wanted me dead, He did not have to use HIV to do it. This illness was not about me. This too would bring Him glory.

It was as though a light was turned on. I had a flashback of the day I was standing in my kitchen thanking God for my life and how good I thought it was.

"You thanked Me because you had everything you wanted in your life, but do you have Me in your life? I have tried to show you that without me you are nothing and can do nothing. You are not in control. It is not about you. I need your attention; it's time for you to get to work for My Kingdom. Your testimony will heal and deliver many."

This is when I understood the saying, "Confession is not a substitute for conversion; service is no substitute for salvation; and religion is no substitute for relationship."

I confessed Christ, but my conversion was on the slow track. I served where I thought was best but was wasting my grace each day that I didn't recognize His Lordship over my life. I went to church but had a shallow relationship with God. Now, I could hear Him calling me to His service. There was no mistaking that the Lord had spoken to my spirit. My life would soon change forever.

CHAPTER THIRTEEN

Can You Hear Me Now?

In December, the Pastor preached a sermon about Naaman. Naaman was a remarkable figure in biblical history, who had to learn humility and obedience. He was a commander of the army of Syria. His master, the King of Syria, saw Naaman as a great and honorable man of courage because the Lord granted him military victories. With all the respect and praise from everyone, the fact remained that he was a leper.

I believe the Lord allowed his army to be victorious so that he could capture the Jewish girl whose testimony would bring the commanding General of Israel's most significant military enemy to biblical faith. Naaman believed that his healing was in Israel. It was out of the respect that the King had for Naaman that he granted his unusual request, to go to Israel for healing.

The King wrote a letter asking that the King of Israel heal his servant. Elisha told the King of Israel to let the General come so that he would know that there was a prophet in Israel.

When Naaman showed up, the prophet, Elisha, did not come out to greet him. He sent a messenger who told Naaman to go and wash in the River Jordan seven times. Naaman wanted the healing to happen immediately, without any action on his part. Then he began to question the instructions of the prophet. Elisha wanted Naaman to understand that his cure would come solely from the sovereign God of Israel. Naaman needed a lesson in humility to allow him to put his trust in the Lord.

The issue here was obedience. Naaman was finally obedient with prompting from his servants and received his healing. He humbly went back to the man of God and confessed that there was no other God but the God of Israel (2 Kings 5:1-19).

Would I do what it took to become whole? Yes. So the journey began. God and I had a covenant. Where there is a covenant, God gives instructions that we must follow entirely and obediently. He is Adonai and has total control. It is a process that gets us to the point of our destiny. We mess up sometimes, but God does not change. He is the same today; He will be the same tomorrow (Hebrews 13:8). We have new mercies every day to begin again and get it right (Lamentations 3:22-23).

The sermon ended with an altar call for people with "the virus" and those standing in the gap for loved ones infected. I felt ashamed only because of the stigma attached to having the disease. Amira was seated next to me. I looked at her and asked, "Would you be okay if I went to the altar?" I asked her because I wanted her to be okay with the fact that everyone would know. Thousands of people watched the telecast. She shook her head and made a path for me to get by.

I believed God would heal me. When the Pastor laid hands on me, I experienced being "slain in the Spirit" for the very first time. When those of us who came to the altar went to the prayer room, I walked right into the arms of Elder Bernice King and Elder Drane, who began to pray for me.

The situation was so surreal. Here stood the daughter of Martin Luther King Jr. praying for me. I had a flashback of being at the March on Washington with my mother, when I was 10-years old, and learning about the struggles of my ancestors. Elder Drane was a young woman who worked alongside me in the tape ministry, years before.

I remember Sylvie, and I prayed for her as she prepared for her ordination interview with the Elders' Council. Not only was she approved for ordination, but she also became the adjutant for Elder Bernice King that began her fulltime career in ministry.

As they prayed, I felt hope come alive again. Maya Angelou said, "I've learned that people will forget what you said, people will forget what you did, but people will never forget how you made them feel." I have to agree.

I wanted complete healing from the Lord. Practicality, however, was God's message in this situation. The first thing I needed to do was begin taking my meds as prescribed. I'd already realized the danger of taking the medication sporadically. Because I felt well, I only took the meds when I thought about it. How contrary was that?

When first diagnosed, I was so upset at the fact that I was not given medication and was horrified at the thought of the disease ravaging my body. Now, I was able to get the medicine and did not take it as prescribed.

I wanted the Lord to heal me so that I would not have to take medication. I did not want to go through the process. It was too much to take a total of 12 pills three times a day. Yes, this was insane thinking. I could have easily been in the category of people who could not afford the medications that would sustain life. Some of the drugs cost upwards of $1500 a month for each 30-day supply. How could any amount of pills be too much to stay alive? I had an undisciplined life.

While in the "slain" state, I realized what I had to do. It was straightforward: Take the medication faithfully every day, as prescribed, and He would heal me. Even with this, it would take almost two years before I would conform completely. I was like Naaman: Why did I have to follow those instructions? Couldn't I do it another way? Why wouldn't God take away the disease?

Experiencing Adonai (God as Master) always brings me back to remembering that He wants me to accept His will and timing, whether I agree with it or not. When I am disobedient, I hold up my blessing. The month that I completed the Lord's instruction, my doctor introduced me to a new medication that allowed me to take only two pills once a day.

My healing didn't come as I envision it. I live with an undetectable viral load. Undetectable means the amount of virus in the blood is so low that a test can't measure it, and it cannot be sexually transmitted. Even when you're undetectable, it's important to keep taking the treatment as prescribed so it can keep fighting the virus to prevent drug resistance. Drug resistance can happen when the virus changes in a way that makes some treatments no longer effective.

I had to learn to be a responsible, active participant in my healing. Almost 25 years later, I'm still here, living an otherwise healthy life. Living with this condition will not be in vain. This is the thorn in my flesh that keeps me humble and reminds me that God's grace is sufficient, and His power is made perfect in my weakness.

PART III

El Shaddai
"Lord God Almighty"

CHAPTER FOURTEEN

Our God is All-Sufficient

To be introduced to God as El Shaddai is incredible and brings a sense of amazement. El Shaddai, we know as the God that is "More than enough." He gives us all we need. El Shaddai will produce what we need as long as we continue to ask because everything we need He can provide. The more we draw on Him, the more He creates for us, as a mother would keep producing nourishment for a child.

El Shaddai is an all-sufficient God that can turn nature around, providing a miracle that is contradictory to natural events.

Yes, God sets natural things into action, but He can supersede all-natural happenings. We see El Shaddai when He gives Abraham and Sarah a son when they are 89 and 99-years old. Giving birth at that age is genuinely against nature.

When Abram was 99-years old, the Lord appeared to Abram and said to him (Genesis 17:1-2), "I am (El Shaddai) Almighty God; walk before Me and be blameless. And I will make My covenant between You and Me, and will multiply you exceedingly" (NKJV).

We see El Shaddai when Jacob asks Laban to allow him to leave with his family and return home. Laban begs him to stay and continue to tend his flocks. El Shaddai performs miracles when Jacob does something that may not have made sense to other people.

In Genesis 30:25-43, Jacob asked Laban to allow him to remove the speckled, spotted and streaked animals from his herd as his wages. Then Jacob took rods of poplar and almond and plane trees, and peeled white stripes in them, exposing the white which was in the rods. He put rods in front of the flocks in the watering troughs, where the animals came to drink and mate. The flocks bore striped, speckled, and spotted offspring.

Jacob separated his herds and did not put them with Laban's flock. When the stronger of the flock were mating, Jacob would place the rods in their sight at the watering troughs, so that they would mate by the rods; but when the flock was feeble, he did not put them in; so the feebler animals were Laban's and the stronger ones belonged to Jacob.

El Shaddai superseded nature and produce speckled, spotted and streaked animals just by them looking at the rods as they mated. Jacob returned to his home, a very wealthy man.

El Shaddai moved once I had a repentant heart after my miscarriage and received another chance to deliver a healthy baby. The tubal ligation was still intact, and I conceived twice. El Shaddai is working in our everyday lives.

We are to be somewhat self-sufficient, able to participate in providing for ourselves, but are never totally autonomous because we are dependent on God, who is all-sufficient. The Lord provides food for the birds, but they don't sit around with their mouths open, waiting for nourishment to fall from the sky. The birds work to get what they need for food and shelter.

In this seventh day, everything we need is already here. We have to learn to access it, just like the birds. God commands us to depend on Him, but not to sit around and do nothing to obtain what we need. We must live by faith responsibly, being careful as we succeed that we don't begin to believe we don't need anyone or anything to survive. More important is to be patient. God fulfills His promises. If we get impatient and start doing things on our own, we find ourselves at a dead-end and out of the will of God.

Twenty-five years had passed for Abraham and Sarah, and God's promise of an heir had not come to pass. Abram decided God was taking too long to fulfill the promise he made and took it upon himself to "help" God by having a child with Hagar. It was another thirteen years before Abram heard from God again and revealed Himself as El Shaddai by providing the child He had promised, with Sarah.

We all have experienced that "back up against the wall" situation where we can only turn to the Lord for help. How many experiences like this must we endure before we realize that He is essential in all that we do?

We cannot obey even one of God's commands with our strength because every command is impossible without a God-generated miracle. Our weakness is in His divine plan.

(John 15:12) This is My commandment that you love one another as I have loved you (NKJV).

(I Corinthians: 4-7) Love suffers long and is kind; love does not envy; love does not parade itself, is not puffed up; does not behave rudely, does not seek its own, is not provoked, thinks no evil; does not rejoice in iniquity, but rejoices in the truth; bears all things, believes all things, hopes all things, endures all things (NKJV).

(Romans 12:14) Bless those who persecute you: bless and do not curse (NKJV).

(Ephesians 4:3) Be kind to one another, tenderhearted, forgiving one another, even as God in Christ forgave you (NKJV).

I don't know about you, but I can't do any of these things in my strength or by my own will. The spirit may be willing, but the flesh is weak. We need God even to understand the scriptures. Only the Spirit of God can turn knowledge into an I-know-it-deep-inside revelation. It is when we conclude that we are helpless that the power of God becomes a certainty in our lives.

As Christians, we should understand that it is our responsibility to participate and play an active role in our spiritual lives. It's the power from the all-sufficient God, El Shaddai, that allows us to fulfill His impossible commands. El Shaddai produces MIRACLES.

(Philippians 2:13) For it is God who works in you both to will and to do for His good pleasure (NKJV).

CHAPTER FIFTEEN

God Doesn't Need Your Help to Fulfill His Promises

It's hard to continually be obedient to God, giving Him total control in every aspect of my life. I thought of myself as a giving person. What I discovered was the understanding of the saying, "You can't beat God at giving."

It is easy to give to our family and friends. I always gave away clothes, supported food/can drive during the holidays, and worked on civic committees. I thought I understood the concept of tithes and offerings to the church. I give my time by being a volunteer to work for church conferences and such.

What the Lord showed me was that these were all calculated moves to satisfy an essential requirement so that I could say

I was concerned and involved. I was not giving money, time, or talent as a sacrifice to glorify God.

Once again, Adonai (Master) showed up, making me face the fact that I had to relinquish my control in that area of my life. The Lord forced me to understand that He allowed me to have the job I had, and He allowed me to make the money I made. It was all His. Not 10 percent, not 50 percent, not 90 percent, but 100 percent was His. He allows us to use His resources.

I was working as a Loan Officer for a major mortgage company in Atlanta in the late 1990s. The company paid a commission for each loan. The number of loans closed in two weeks determined my commission. Some paydays were more significant than others. This particular payday, my check was exceptionally substantial. From experience, I learned to pay our bills in advance when I received a considerable paycheck. I knew there would be paydays when my check was not so great. With this particular check, I decided to pay our mortgage in advance for three months.

I purchased a cashier's check (certified funds) because I knew that if I left the money in my checking account, a new dress or pair of shoes would start to look better than paying bills in advance. After purchasing the cashiers' check, I drove to my company's corporate office in Dunwoody, Georgia. As I was getting out of my car, I remembered the cashiers' check and decided to take it with me into the office so that I could mail it to my mortgage company.

After several hours of working, I decided to pack up to leave the office. I then looked for the check to put it in an envelope so that I could drop it in the outgoing mail as I left the building. I looked in my case, and there was no check. Since I carried a lot of paperwork, I thought the cashier's check must be among all the papers. It was getting late, and I didn't want to be stuck in traffic on I-285 during rush hour, so I left without finding the check. I figured I could look for it later at home.

That night while watching TV, I remembered that I needed to look for the check. I went to my room and got my laptop case and emptied it on the floor, and went through every piece of paper. There was no check. I went out to my car and searched it through and through. No check. I became a little antsy. After a few deep breaths, I thought, tomorrow, I will just call the bank and tell them to put a stop payment on the check and issue me another check.

I did not sleep well and could hardly wait until 9:00 a.m. At the stroke of 9:00, I called my bank. I spoke with one of the bank managers, Princess Leigh (yes, that her real name). I was unprepared for what she was about to tell me. The bank could put a stop payment on the check, but for the bank to re-issue a cashiers' check, I would have to get a bond for the check amount before they could give me a replacement. The drama began.

Ms. Leigh gave me the phone number of a bonding company that the bank dealt with previously. The person who answered the phone at the bonding company was an incredibility rude woman who informed me that I would have to make an appointment to come into their office and fill out an application and pay for a credit report and a background investigation. The fee for the bond depended on the amount of the check. The higher the check amount, the higher the cost would be. This process could take 30 days or more. I was devastated.

My next thought was, "I need to talk to God." I told God that I would not believe that He would bless me with the ability to make that amount of money, and then it would be lost. I was a tither at my church; I believed the scripture continuously preached.

(Malachi 3:8-10) *"Will a man rob God? Yet you have robbed Me! But you say, 'In what way have we robbed You?' In tithes and offerings. You are cursed with a curse, for you have robbed Me, even this whole nation. Bring all the tithes into the storehouse, that there may be food in My house, and try Me now in this,"* says the Lord of hosts, *"If I will not open for you the windows of heaven and pour out for you such blessing that there will not be room enough to receive" (NKJV).*

How could He allow this to happen? Was this a curse from God?

During my time in prayer, I received the revelation of a couple of things. I remembered my thoughts and actions of the previous day. When leaving the bank, I received a call from my friend, Connie. Connie was the coordinator for a group of us planning a cruise to the Bahamas. She needed the balance of the money for my trip. I had forgotten the date the balance was due. I wished she had called before I purchase the cashier's check for three months mortgage payment, two months would have worked as well. I thought I'd only pay half my tithe and make it up at the end of the month." BINGO, there it was.

God said, "How dare you think about your selfish needs over my kingdom. I want to trust you with so much more."

I was immediately repentant and begged God's forgiveness. God had been so good to me. It was not like I did not have the money for the trip without paying my tithe. I just wanted to use the other money for something else.

The church did so much in our community. We were building a 10,000-seat cathedral, family life center, senior citizens' home subdivision, and many other community projects on the 240 acres purchased by our church for our 25,000 membership and community. I knew this was fertile soil in which to plant my seeds.

I promised God, from that moment on, I would always try to be a good steward over every blessing He gave me.

But He wasn't finished.

The Lord showed me that my giving, or the amount I was giving, wasn't the issue as much as neglecting to put Him first. No, there was no curse for not giving ten percent, but there was no blessing for being disobedient. Honoring God, foremost, had to be my agenda in everything.

I became free from the bondage that made me feel insufficient when I couldn't give ten percent. I remembered that time all I had to offer was $1.75, and faith in God. El Shaddai had blessed me so mightily. There is so much freedom in giving according to how God blesses me.

Dorian had a doctor's appointment that morning. After dropping him off at the doctor, I went back to the corporate office since it was in the same area. My loan processor, Laura, and I began once again looking for the check. We went through her desk and the desk I worked from the day before. No check. I called the bank again and told Ms. Leigh what the bonding company had told me. I did not want to go through all the rigmarole, and I did not want to wait 30 days or more.

Princess told me to come into the bank, and she would see what she could do. She did not sound very hopeful. As I hung up the phone with her, Dorian's doctor called. They were admitting Dorian into the hospital. As I packed my things, Laura told me that she had been to a couple of yard sales the previous weekend and found a Louis Vuitton shopping bag that was practically brand new and asked me if I wanted it.

"Of course," I said. Laura told me that she would walk me out to the parking lot and get the bag out of her truck. As we came out of the lobby, we went out of the side exit of the office building, which leads directly out to the parking lot. As we walked, Laura startled me as she turned quickly to the right. I turned to see what she turned to see. We stopped dead in our tracks. About five feet away, in a bush, was an envelope. Neither one of us said anything. It couldn't be! We were in an outdoor parking lot of an office building full of employees going in and out all day. It had been twenty-four hours since I lost the check. We ran over to the bush. Citizens Trust Bank glared at me from the envelope.

I grabbed the envelope that was sitting there on a branch as though it was a letter holder. It wasn't wrinkled, dirty, or disturbed in any way. While holding my breath, I opened the envelope. There it was, the cashier's check. I shouted and jumped up and down. I thanked God, for it was a miracle, a "burning bush experience." El Shaddai spoke to me loud and clear. "I AM WHO I AM." We are dependent on Him, and service to Him comes first before anything.

Laura stood there in awe. She had chills all over her body. I asked her if she believed in the power of God, and she said, "Yes!" El Shaddai revealed Himself as the God who I am dependent on, who can perform miracles that will get us where we need to be in Christ.

CHAPTER SIXTEEN

My Revelation About Giving

I've come to believe that Jesus Christ made us free from the curse of the law (Galatians 3:10-13). I don't believe that God will curse us for not bringing a tithe (10%) of our income to the church, but I do think that it is through our financial support that we prepare the Church for service. If we do not give as Christ has commanded, it will keep our churches in financial bondage and will not permit the Church to complete the work of Christ on earth. We must realize the fullness of our freedom in Christ. It doesn't matter what side of the tithing debate (law versus grace) you're on, giving to fulfill the work of the Kingdom is a command from God.

Not only that, but God inspires us to be substantial in giving:

(2 Corinthians 9:10-13) Now may He who supplies seed to the sower, and, bread for food, supply and multiply the seed you

have sown and increase the fruits of your righteousness, while you are enriched in everything for all liberality, which causes thanksgiving through us to God. For the administration of this service not only supplies the needs of the saints, but also is abounding through many thanksgivings to God, while, through the proof of this ministry, they glorify God for the obedience of your confession to the gospel of Christ, and for your liberal sharing with them and all men (NKJV).

We are blessed when we give cheerfully:

(2 Corinthians 9:6-9) But this I say: He who sows sparingly will also reap sparingly, and he who sows bountifully will also reap bountifully. So, let each one give as he purposes in his heart, not grudgingly or of necessity; for God loves a cheerful giver. And God is able to make all grace abound toward you, that you, always having all sufficiency in all things, may have an abundance for every good work. As it is written: He has dispersed abroad, He has given to the poor; His righteousness endures forever (NKJV).

We should give financial support to our pastors:

(1 Corinthians 9:13-14) Do you not know that those who minister the holy things eat of the things of the temple, and those who serve at the altar partake of the offerings of the altar? Even so, the Lord has commanded that those who preach the Gospel should live from the Gospel (NKJV).

CHAPTER SEVENTEEN

God Wants Us to Prosper So We Can Be a Blessing

Elohim has created us and is in covenant with us. Adonai is Lord and Master and is in total control of His creations. El Shaddai is all-sufficient. He will give us direction and instruction as well as protect and provide for us in all areas of our lives, including our finances. We have to allow money to flow through us. If we hoard cash for ourselves, it will run out. If we let it flow through us, then it will continue to flow.

Every seed planted in good soil will reap a harvest. There are principles to "reaping a harvest." God expects us to ask Him how much to give. When He tells us what to offer, we need to be obedient, not giving more or less than what He specifies. No man should be able to pressure us into giving or make us feel guilty when we don't have a specific amount more than our offering.

There will be times when God urges us to give a sacrificial offering. To me, this means a "sacrifice of our desires" (self-sacrifice), not a sacrifice of the mortgage or car payment, but giving up something we desire for the greater good. We relinquish a desire, not a necessity, like bringing a brown bag lunch to work rather than eating out in a restaurant or rent a movie and make popcorn rather than go to the theater.

God also wants us to understand that we should give desiring a definite result from Him. A miracle always accompanies the increase of any seed back to us. All miracles operate by faith. When we give without the desired result in mind, we do not give in faith.

Penny's young son got into trouble and went to prison for a couple of years. She was a widow and lived on a fixed income. Of course, she prayed for her only child to turn his life around once he was released. It was at her homegoing that her Pastor revealed how much faith she had that God would answer her prayer. Every week when she gave her offering, it would be accompanied by an additional dollar and a note on the envelope that said, "This is my sacrifice to you Lord because I know you will save my son." Her son sat on the front row that day with tears in his eyes, as a college graduate with a good job. Penny gave a sacrificial offering expecting a desired result from God.

(Hebrews 11:1) Now faith is the substance of things hoped for, the evidence of things not seen (NKJV).

We should also understand the term "more than enough." Some Christians believe that they should only look to receive precisely enough to take care of their own needs. The Bible does not say this. In 2 Corinthians 9:8, it says, *"And God is able to make all grace abound toward you, that you, always having all sufficiency in all things, may have an abundance for every good work" (NKJV).*

The generous, obedient giver will not lack but will have more than enough to be a blessing to others. Yes, God will give us much so that we can give away much. How can we clothe the naked if we can only clothe ourselves? How can we possibly feed others if we get only enough for ourselves to eat? I cannot count the number of times that I have cooked Sunday dinner for a few friends, and more people show up than anticipated. There was always food left-over, regardless of how many people ate dinner.

When I volunteer my talents, I place value on what I deposit. I make sure that what I do is for the betterment of the project, that people can see the excellence of God. I believe God, in certain instances, has me give more in talents and time than money because the gifts and resources He has given to me can do more to advance the Kingdom at that time. We can't throw money at a situation when your time (which is a valuable commodity because you can never get it back), is what the Lord would have you spend for the Kingdom.

Lacking foresight in time of giving will put us in a very unpleasant place of insufficiency when it is time to harvest. We should plan to support God's work because we know what God's plan is for us.

"For I know the plans I have for you," declares the LORD, "plans to prosper you and not to harm you, plans to give you hope and a future" (Jeremiah 29:11 NIV).

When you have no finances, you will have to do without and not be able to bless others. We all know people who never have money or are not available when it's time to give. It is not because God does not want to bless them with money to give. The reason is that they are not givers when they have money. I've learned that people use their time and money for what is important to them. God never promised to give seed to the Christian. He promised to provide seed to the sower (2 Corinthians 9:10).

The Law of the Harvest is Irrevocable

The principles of the law of the harvest, just as gravity, are in effect whether we recognize them or not.

These principles are permanent, and no one can escape them. Every harvest begins with a seed, be it time, talents, finances, deeds, thoughts, or words.

I remember reading a story about a woman who made quilts to give to the sick and shut-inn. She became ill and couldn't pay her bills. Many people came to visit and brought items they had made. Her adult son asked her church to help with her bills as she had been a member for many years. When asked whether his mother gave financially to the church, his response was, "Oh, no, we don't give money; she only has enough to care for herself." She reaped her harvest of visits and homemade items.

If you plant oranges, you will harvest oranges. If you plant apples, you will harvest apples. You will never plant oranges and harvest apples. Planting seeds in fertile soil is most important. Fertile soil is where God is using His people to fulfill His will. We should plant a variety of seeds to be able to harvest many different things we will need to perform the will of God.

We should remember to sow what God instructs to give. There is a thin line between faith and foolishness. Being a good steward over your finances will make you a cheerful giver. We cannot be cheerful about giving if we listen to any other voice than the Lord's. If God said it, then He will provide for it.

If we are faithful to plant more out of the abundance, we will reap more. The more seed we plant, the more harvest is received, and the more we are expected to give. We can provide even more out of our overflow. Giving to the physical church is just a part of our service. It is outside the walls of the church that we must also plant seeds.

Even the world knows and uses these principles; think about the banking system. When you put your money into savings accounts, money market account, or CDs, it provides the banks with the capital to make loans to help other people. You are effectively lending money to the bank and are paid interest for doing so. You get more back than you deposited initially. The more you deposit, the more interest you receive. There is a waiting period before you can reap the benefit. The longer the wait time usually, the higher the benefit.

(Galatians 6:7-8) says, *"Do not be deceived, God is not mocked; for whatever a man sows, that he will also reap. For he who sows to his flesh will of the flesh reap corruption, but he who sows to the Spirit will of the Spirit reap everlasting life "(NKJV).*

Spiritual investments are crucial to our daily lives. Sowing and reaping is a part of life; it's about seeds planted. The good seed is the Word of God. *(1 Peter 1:23) Having been born again, not of corruptible seed but incorruptible, through the word of God which lives and abides forever (NKJV).*

God's word is the good seed we need to plant not only in our hearts but in the hearts of those we encounter each day. The good seed is incorruptible. When we make spiritual investments by planting or depositing good seeds by what we say, and by our actions, we will produce an incorruptible harvest.

My involvement with AID Atlanta as an HIV Prevention Counselor is a time investment of sharing information with college students and women. My goal is to encourage unaffected people (Primarily heterosexual women who in 2017 made up 86% of new cases) to take precautionary measures and those affected to be part of ending the epidemic by preventing the virus from being passed to others. My role also provides me the opportunity to minister to those fearful of facing life with an incurable illness.

Acts of kindness are no small thing. It is a good seed that harvests amazing fruit both in our lives and the lives of those around us and is easy to incorporate into our daily lives when we have more than enough.

I go to the same nail shop each time I get my nails manicured. I asked my manicurist Nina one day if she would help me perform acts of kindness, and she was more than willing. I leave her money ($7) to pay for an eyebrow arch. She would choose a person she felt needed uplifting, and at the end of their service, she would hand them an envelope with the cash for the service and a note that read: God cares for you! "Whoever pursues righteousness and kindness will find life, righteousness, and honor" (Proverbs21:21 ESV). The smiling face of her customer would be shared on Facebook to inspire others.

I never forgot the cashier who swiped her credit card for a remaining balance on my grocery bill when I forgot my wallet. While picking up a few items at Publix, I saw a bouquet of beautiful flowers. I decided to buy them and give them to the cashier. I knew she would not remember me or her perfect good deed. When she rang up my items, she remarked that the flowers were beautiful. She told me she purchased a beautiful vase but never had time to buy flowers to put in it. What a set-up. When she finished bagging my groceries, I handed her the flowers and said, "This is for you, God loves the cheerful giver you are." I guess I wasn't the only one who felt that way because her co-workers began to applaud.

A desire to do more came to me as I read about a woman who wanted to start a chapter of the Awesome Foundation in Atlanta. Once I read the great things that were happening all over the world through his grassroots organization, I was ready, but was this a good thing or a God thing? My year commitment as a trustee entailed a contribution of $100 a month along with nine other trustees, selecting and awarding an individual or organization that is making a meaningful impact in the community with a $1000 grant. I checked with the Source to be sure. It was going to be a sacrifice, so I planned out my giving of time and resources.

After the selection of the first awardee, I became more confident that I planted in good soil. The grant recipient was a teacher assigned to a Title 1 school that assists students at risk of failure, living in or near poverty. This teacher donated every single article of clothing he owned, only leaving one outfit. He wore that one outfit for 90 days to raise uniforms for kids that attend Title 1 schools who wear the same thing every single day because they lack resources in their closets at home. He did this to show the severity of kids who struggle with limited access to clean clothes.

During the journey, he raised over 200 uniforms but had nowhere to store the items. The grant allowed him to purchase the wood and materials needed to build "Closets of Hope." These closets serve as a way for under-resourced schools to provide clean clothes to students who lack. It would also serve as an encourager to students who disconnect from their lesson because of their attire.

After ten months of awarding grants to similar incredible projects, what I thought as a sacrifice at first became such a blessing. The board of trustees is an amazingly diverse group of people, and it was not hard to commit for another year.

Accessing our resources is how we also reap our harvest. Look around you and take inventory of people who have the resources or knowledge that you need.

In recognizing and the resources that surround me, I take a good look at things I desire to accomplish and create a list. Jehovah is the source, so first things first. I pray that my actions would be in His will, then I look for the resource, someone, or something that God put in my life that can help me achieve my goal.

For example, I have been working with Mark for more than ten years. He is a videographer who accompanies me when we travel to conduct oral history interviews. We spend a minimum of a week together driving to interview locations. I believe we have gotten to know each other well and chat about our lives outside of work.

I wanted to invest in a few stocks I heard about, didn't have a clue on how to go about this. Yes, I could have hired someone, but after losing money in 2008, when the stock market went haywire, I wanted to be hands-on and more in control of my investments. Mark came to mind because in a couple of our conversations during the years, he told me of how as a young man, he made some mistakes and found himself sleeping in his car.

Once he got himself together, completed school, found work, and was financially stable, he began to invest in stocks and created other streams of income. Never again did Mark want to be economically unstable.

I called Mark and told him what I wanted to do, and within an hour, he walked me through creating E-Trade and Robinhood brokerage accounts. He gave me sound advice and references to websites to help me better understand buying and selling stocks.

I can't say it enough, God is the Source, and your Re-sources are available to you, but they won't fall in your lap. We have to access them. A word of advice. Don't be discouraged when who or what you thought was a resource doesn't give you what you need. Could be that the time for that harvest hasn't come yet. Move on to the next one and never leave a stone unturned because of preconceived notions about a person or situation. All your resources come from God, but all your resources are not Christian or look like you.

Sometimes we don't get it right. When we find ourselves in a position of not enough or without a harvest, we have to go back to the Source and figure out where we went wrong.

Knowledge, understanding, and application of the principles of sowing and reaping have been such a blessing in my life. Every seed that grows has a miracle attached to it. It's encountering El Shaddai, as He performs supernaturally.

CHAPTER EIGHTEEN

Father Knows Best

It was 2000, a new year, a new decade, and life was on an upswing, except I had an earache, which needed immediate medical attention. The series of events that would lead to the end of this drama would change my life forever.

I have always had a problem with my ears if I allowed water to get into them. During one of my beauty shop appointments, while getting my hair shampooed, water must have gotten in my ear. The next thing I knew, I was suffering from an earache that felt as though someone was holding a torch in my inner ear.

I called Dr. Dockery's office, the most magnificent ear, nose, and throat specialist in Atlanta. There is an art form needed to master getting an appointment to see him in an emergency. I had convinced the nurse that my ear canal felt as though it was on fire. I simply told her that I would either die or kill someone because the pain was unbearable. I needed to see the doctor right away. She was compassionate and made an appointment for the very next morning.

The doctor relieved the pain by putting a small wick of cotton soaked with pain medication way down in my ear canal. I received a prescription for some wonder drug that stopped the pain immediately. He instructed me to come back the following week to have the wick removed. My scheduled appointment conflicted with one of my client appointments. I tried to reschedule my appointment and would be on hold with the office for long periods.

My schedule was so busy that I didn't have the time to hold on indefinitely. I had no pain, so there was no urgency to get back to the doctor. Days and days went by. Then the pain was back again, ten times worse.

Once again, I called the doctor and waited on hold forever. Finally, I got through and was able to plead my case once again to get an appointment the next day. Bright and early the following day, I was in the doctor's office.

After the doctor got over the fact that I waited so long to come back and get the wick removed, he tried to remove it. It would not budge. The pain was a gut-wrenching pain that made me sick to my stomach. The doctor could put some type of drops in my ear to try to soften the wick. Still, it would not move. With another prescription and another appointment for a couple of days later, I made my way home. I would not make the same mistake by missing the next office visit. I would have to drive to the Buckhead office in Atlanta. As much pain as I was in, I would have driven to Alaska.

The night before my appointment, I was in total agony. I prayed that I would be able to make it through the night. The blaze in my ear had my whole head throbbing. Dorian called his job at the correctional facility and told them that he would be taking the next morning off so that he could go with me to the doctor's office.

Finally, it was morning. Dorian got up, and we agreed that he would take Micah to Rainbow Park Baptist Academy, where he attended preschool. I got out of bed, showered, and dressed, knowing that it was going to take a while for me to accomplish this because the inferno in my ear had me at my wit's end. A trip to Micah's school should be twenty minutes round trip. I wanted to be ready when Dorian returned.

I had to be at the doctor's office at 10:00 a.m. It was 7:55 when Dorian left the house. There was plenty of time before we had to leave. Since there were going to be two people in the car as we drove into Atlanta, we could whip downtown in the HOV lane reserved for multiple riders and carpools, avoiding most of the morning rush-hour traffic. We would be there in forty minutes, tops.

I had never been to this office, having always visited the office in Decatur. The receptionist gave me excellent directions. (No GPS at this time) I was sure I could find the office, park the car, and be prompt for this appointment that would end my agony.

Fully dressed, I tried to wait patiently for Dorian's return. I did not want to be late. After all, Dorian was only accompanying me. I still had to drive myself. Dorian had his driver's license suspended for a DUI. I had to drive him everywhere, even to and from work, regardless of what shift he worked.

Some mornings it would be rise and shine and get him to work by 5:00 a.m. He was a supervisor, and the sergeant had to be on the post an hour before the shift began. When he worked this shift, it interrupted my day. I would drive him to work in my nightgown. Once back at home, I would try to go back to sleep until it was time for me to get Raheem up and out to school and prepare for my departure to my office.

Just as I got my momentum flowing at my desk, it would be time to make the 15-mile trip to pick Dorian up from work and take him home. With that done, I would return to my office to complete my day. I resented this chore, and I began to resent him.

Since Dorian no longer had the responsibility of driving, his feeble attempts at trying to stay sober seemed to dwindle.

It seemed so unfair that I suffered more than he did. At 9:45 a.m. I am waiting by the front door, praying that the police wouldn't stop him. I was so dumb. I shouldn't have let him drive, but I was in so much pain.

That's when I saw our GMC Jimmy start to pull slowly into the driveway. Relief ran through me. I opened the door, and I watched him back out as though he was going to drive away when he saw me. He stopped and pulled back into the driveway. I came down the front steps of the house. By this time, I was furious. He had only gotten out of bed two hours before.

He still had on his pajamas under a pair of jeans he threw on. He couldn't be drunk. Could he have taken pills that could have taken effect that fast? I walked up to the truck and asked him, "What took you so long?"

"Traffic," he tells me.

I told him to get out of the truck.

He began to tell me that it was trash day and that I needed to go into the house and get the trash can.

I then became outraged. The pain in my ear felt like it was going to make my head split wide open. If I raced all the way Atlanta, I might just make my doctor's appointment on time. I could not believe he was talking about the trash. I had not taken the trash out in years. Why would I do it now, with this terrible pain? I couldn't understand.

"Just get out of the truck," I told him.

As he got out, I realized something was not quite right. I jumped in the driver's seat and backed out of the driveway. When I got to the top of the driveway, I looked back to where he was standing, and an odd feeling ran through me. He was standing there in front of the downstairs door, looking around, bewildered.

It was the same faraway look I saw in his eyes some weeks before. It was as though he wasn't in the reality of this world. He sat on the bed, staring into space. At that time, I asked the Lord, "How can you be a compassionate and loving God if you will allow him to continue to live that way?"

His quality of life was near zero. I wanted God to move on his behalf. He was only going through the motions, day by day. Like a functioning alcoholic, he was able to work without incident at the job, but once he left work, it was a different story.

Without breaking all the speed limits, I drove to Piedmont Road and found a parking garage right next to Dr. Dockery's office building. I ran through the lobby to the elevators. I dashed into the waiting room, straight to the receptionist's desk to check-in. Five minutes later, I was sitting in the exam chair, waiting for the doctor to see me. My stomach was doing a loop-de-loop.

The medical assistant came into the room with a tray of instruments. When I saw the long tweezers-type tool, I felt faint. That was the culprit that caused so much pain the last time the Doctor tried to remove the wick from my ear.

The doctor entered the room. Was I sweating? It was January. The doctor put on his gloves as he asked me, "Are you ready?"

I replied, "Yes."

He picked up the long tweezers, pulled my ear open, and inserted the tweezers. In an instant, it was out. It was amazing. The pain immediately stopped. He dropped a tiny dark brown hardball on the tray next to the exam chair. It was unimaginable that something that small could cause so much pain.

I left the doctor's office with a song in my heart because I felt like a new person. I wasn't even mad at Dorian anymore. I decided to drive through Buckhead and go to my favorite little wholesale shopping area in midtown.

After a short time of browsing shoes at the shoe warehouse, I settled for a black leather purse that was on sale. Delighted with my purchase, I left the store and took the scenic route back to Decatur. Once in my neighborhood, I decided to stop and buy the fixings for a nice lunch. I would be kind to Dorian. I thought about the conference I attended where P.B. Wilson spoke. I needed to make a "touchdown" today.

As I pulled into the Publix parking lot, I was still smiling. I bought spiced ham, Italian bread, sliced yellow American cheese, and dill pickles. These were all Dorian's favorites for making a hero sandwich. I still couldn't get over how great I felt.

Driving the few short blocks to my house, I didn't get that sinking feeling I usually got when it was time for me to go home, knowing Dorian had been there all day alone. Most of the time, I never knew what I would find when I arrived home. It wasn't until I turned into the driveway that the sinking feeling returned.

The downstairs door to the house was wide open. I went in very slowly. I called out to Dorian, but there was no answer. I walked up the stairs, still calling his name. I looked in the kitchen and living room. Finally, I am standing in the doorway of our bedroom. There was Dorian, passed out on the floor.

How many times had I gone through this scenario? I was so mad. Not angry, MAD. I was ready to explode. I screamed out to God. "Why, Lord? Why?" I could not believe that I would have to continue to live this way. I'd had all I could take. I went to my closet and found my video camera. I videotaped him lying there. I taped over his favorite movie, "The Mummy." I figured that would make him mad.

I got close to his face. I remember thinking that he was so out of it that his face pressed deeply into the carpet. My foot touched him, and he didn't flinch. I was going to use this video to show his doctor the way he was abusing pain meds and alcohol. I wanted someone to see what my family and I were going through each day.

I went to the phone in the kitchen and called my friend and prayer partner, Sylvie. I needed someone to listen to me, someone to pray with me. I told her that I could not take it anymore. He would have to leave. I hated coming home, not knowing what I might find. I filled her in on what had transpired that morning, and I went on and on and on.

She let me vent until I ran out of steam. She then began to encourage me, and then we prayed, and it settled my spirit. After we finished praying, she jokingly said to me, "You better check to make sure he is not dead."

I said, "If he is not, I'm going to kill him."

After hanging up the phone, I walked back into the bedroom. Dorian was still lying there on the floor. He had so much to live for: A month before, Dorian's viral load was "undetectable." This feat was occurring for a person that could have full-blown AIDS. He just could not cope with his illness and the guilt that he had passed it on to me, so he self-medicated and drank.

I went into the bathroom and closed the door. I sat on the side of the tub and began asking God questions. I remember thinking, "Lord, how can you continue to allow him to live in such a state? You are supposed to be a merciful God. Why Lord! Why!"

It had been a year since I wrote in my journal what the Lord had spoken to me. "If Dorian did not change his life, he was going to die."

I know God told me that. I wrote it in my journal, but I didn't want to believe it. I mentioned it to my friend, Cookie, and she said, to me, "God could not have told you that!"

I could not believe I would have to bury another husband. I was too young to be a widow twice. Sitting there, begging the Lord to please give me the strength to deal with the situation, I was weary, so very, very tired. I could not go any further in my strength alone. As much as I loved Dorian, I was ready for the life of a never-ending, roller-coaster ride to stop.

Raheem, then 12-years old, came home from school. He entered the bedroom as I came out of the bathroom. He stopped in amazement of his father lying there on the floor.

He had seen his father like this before, but each time he would look at him in disbelief.

Raheem asked me what was going on. I told him that I found his father like that when I came home. We both stood there for a minute, looking at Dorian.

Raheem then said, "Mom, let's at least get him off the floor and put him on the bed."

I agreed. I bent down, and Raheem says to me, "Is he breathing?"

I looked at him very carefully but could not tell. I lifted his head and turned him over. Panic gripped me as I looked into his face. His nose was running, and his mouth partially opened with white saliva coming from it. I screamed, "Call 911."

Raheem dialed the number and handed me the phone. I began telling the operator what had occurred. She asked if I had administered CPR.

I said, "No."

She told me what to do. I wiped Dorian's mouth and attempted to open it. His jaw was locked, and his teeth clenched together.

Dorian was dead.

I heard the operator say that she would send help.

Much of what happened after that is blurry. The Fire Department showed up first. They came in and determined that there was nothing that they could do and left. The police and ambulance were next. They asked several questions and called the medical examiner's office.

The medical examiner asked questions that got me angry all over again because I had been pleading with Dorian's doctor to cut back on the medication prescribed for him. He was addicted to prescription drugs, but I could not get anyone to hear me. They had acknowledged that Dorian had been to several different hospital emergency rooms to get different doctors to give him prescriptions for pain meds. He was on the pharmacy alert list. He was only able to get his medication through a pain management center, but he was still on too much medicine.

His life was one big fog. That was the reason I took the video. I was going to show his doctor that Dorian was abusing the meds. I listed the medications for the medical examiner. He had been prescribed Ambien for sleeping; antidepressants, Buspar and Paxil; muscle relaxers, Flexeril and Soma; and Oxycontin, Vicodin or Lortab for pain. Even the Medical Examiner was astonished at the list.

I rang Sylvie back. "Girl, you are not going to believe this. I went to my bedroom, and Dorian was dead." At that point, I broke down.

There was silence on the other end. Sylvie told me to stay calm; she was on her way over to my house.

He was in the bedroom about four hours before they wrapped him in a sheet and carried him out. They took his body to the medical examiner's office. I felt so down.

The roller coaster came to a halt. Life was over for a fun-loving, good guy, who could not get it together and trust God for healing and total restoration. He chose to stay in a numbed state of being. Everyone liked him, but no one truly knew the hell my family and I had to endure because of his addictions. He helped anyone he could and was well-respected by his coworkers and staff. Before his work could begin to suffer, he took steps to retire. He was 30 days short of having enough time to retire. His co-workers admired him enough to volunteer to give him their vacation time to help him get the hours needed for him to retire. His retirement would have begun the very next week. With all the disease and addiction struggles we went through, it was ironic that he would die of a heart attack.

The military homegoing was emotional. No one could believe that Dorian was gone. Jason, his oldest and dearest friend, spoke about him in a way no one else could have. His co-workers took up most of the seats in the chapel. They, too, expressed their heartfelt sorrow. It was standing room only. The United States Army presented me with an American flag in remembrance of his service in Vietnam, as did the Department of Corrections for his years of dedication as a sergeant for the Department.

El Shaddai surely is the lover of my soul. He kept me close when Derrick died. He kept me when Mary died. When I found myself a single parent once again, overwhelmed by loneliness, and the financial need was great, I could do nothing but expect the Lord to step in, and He did. The Lord reveals himself as a miracle worker over and over again.

PART IV

Yahweh (Jehovah) "The Most Sacred Name"

CHAPTER NINETEEN

Self-existent and a Faithful God

(Exodus 3:15) Moreover God said to Moses, "Thus you shall say to the children of Israel: 'The LORD God of your fathers, the God of Abraham, the God of Isaac, and the God of Jacob, has sent me to you. This is My name forever, and this is My memorial to all generations (NKJV).

Jehovah is the most sacred personal name of God. The reverence of His divine name led to avoiding its use for fear that the Holy name would be misused. The Hebrews used "Adonai" (Lord and Master) instead.

"I AM WHO I AM." He is the "self-existent" God. God was not created. No one and nothing brought Him into existence. He is not dependent on anyone or anything outside Himself for His being.

The name of Jehovah speaks to His faithfulness towards us. His promises of eternal life (John 3:16) an escape from hell;

limitless forgiveness (Romans 5:20); divine wisdom (James 1:2-3,5); and a home with Him when we depart this earth (2 Corinthians 5:6-8). These are enough reasons to be devoted to Him. Humans have a finite mind, so it's hard to understand an infinite God. We strengthen our faith when we recognize that we are dependent on something greater than ourselves rather than something equal to ourselves. Jehovah is the God that will break us down for our good.

As our Creator, He has the right to shape our lives as He sees fit. He can give us, withhold, take away, anything He considers best for our welfare. Submitting to God's will for our lives is very hard at times. Education, social status, or political clout sometimes makes us think highly of ourselves. Continually staying before the Lord will keep us humble; otherwise, the Lord may allow illness or disease, financial ruin, or public disgrace to make us less reliant on ourselves and more in need of Him.

When we empty ourselves, we acknowledge our weaknesses and make room for God's power to fill us. When God allows us to be in a hopeless situation, He wants to reveal His power so that He will receive the glory.

Paul says in 2 Corinthians 12:7-10, "*Therefore, in order to keep me from becoming conceited, I was given a thorn in my flesh, a messenger of Satan, to torment me. Three times I pleaded with the Lord to take it away from me. But he said to me, "My grace is sufficient for you, for My power is made perfect in weakness." Therefore, I will boast all the more gladly about my weaknesses, so that Christ's power may rest on me. That is why, for Christ's sake, I delight in weaknesses, in insults, in hardships, in persecutions, in difficulties. For when I am weak, then I am strong*" (NKJV).

Jehovah is a faithful God, who will always keep His promises, even when we are disobedient. Often we fail to obey His commands, but our salvation stays intact. Disobedience keeps us from experiencing all the blessings God has for us.

* * *

As with the spotted, speckled animals in the story of Laban and Jacob, I have had God tell me to do things that I thought were crazy. Once, I heard God say to go away and listen for Him to speak. The next thing I knew, I was in Cancun, Mexico, with a strong desire to go scuba diving. Scuba diving was something I would never think to do because I don't like large bodies of water. I can swim, but I feel more comfortable in the pool. In the ocean, not so much.

Once in Cancun, I looked for an outing where I could learn to scuba dive in a controlled environment. As it happens, my friend Tricia and I decided to take an excursion to Xcaret, Mexico, which is about 45 minutes away from Cancun. I noticed a sign for a scuba diving trip once we were there. I thought this was perfect and signed up.

The next thing I knew, I am in full scuba-diving gear, wet suit and all, scared to death to dive into the ocean. After instruction from the guide, I plunged 40 feet into the sea. As a group, we swam to destinations that showcased the beautiful coral and plant life. The feeling of being in a dream is what I remember. Beautiful schools of fish surrounded me, but as I reached out, they seemed to disappear as though they weren't real.

It was mystifying. It was calming. Then, as it happened, my weight belt became unbalanced, and I began to twirl a bit. It was as though I was in a fight with something invisible. My wrist touched a plant that stung me. I began to panic a bit and decided to surface. Remembering the rules of not going up too fast, I slowly rose to the surface, to find the water very choppy.

I swam to the boat to find that I was not the first one to come back onboard. I felt as though I experienced something like spiritual warfare, something you must fight, but you can't see it. Things are not what they seem, and an attack can happen at any moment. We must prepare by gaining the knowledge of how to come out of it, even if it's with a few bruises.

The next day, as I lie on the beach looking up into the sun-filled, blue sky, I noticed people parasailing. I got a nudge to try it. I felt as though God was saying, "Meet me up high."

I said, "Lord, you are so funny to me."

I got up, and the next thing I know, I am so high in the sky, marveling over how majestic the view appeared from on high. I literally felt a tap on my shoulder. I was so focused on the beauty of it all, and I forgot why I was up there. I heard God say, "Stay in the high place."

Obedience to do whatever God says, regardless of how silly or crazy we think it is, will always be what's best for us. Most of the time, the benefit of obedience won't be so apparent right away. We have to trust that God will never let us down.

PART V

Yahweh Yireh (Jehovah Jireh) "The Lord Will Provide"

CHAPTER TWENTY

Lord My Provider

(Genesis 22:1-19) Now it came to pass after these things that God tested Abraham, and said to him, "Abraham!" And he said, "Here I am."

Then He said, "Take now your son, your only son, Isaac, whom you love, and go to the land of Moriah, and offer him there as a burnt offering on one of the mountains of which I shall tell you."

So Abraham rose early in the morning and saddled his donkey, and took two of his young men with him and Isaac his son; and he split the wood for the burnt offering and arose and went to the place of which God had told him. Then on the third day Abraham lifted his eyes and saw the place afar off. And Abraham said to his young men, "Stay here with the donkey; the lad and I will go yonder and worship, and we will come back to you."

So Abraham took the wood of the burnt offering and laid it on Isaac, his son; and he took the fire in his hand and a knife, and the two of them went together. But Isaac spoke to Abraham, his father, and said, "My father!"

And he said, "Here I am, my son."

Then he said, "Look, the fire and the wood, but where is the lamb for a burnt offering?"

And Abraham said, "My son, God will provide for Himself the lamb for a burnt offering." So the two of them went together.

Then they came to the place of which God had told him. And Abraham built an altar there and placed the wood in order; and he bound Isaac his son and laid him on the altar, upon the wood. And Abraham stretched out his hand and took the knife to slay his son.

But the Angel of the Lord called to him from heaven and said, "Abraham, Abraham!"

So he said, "Here I am."

And He said, "Do not lay your hand on the lad, or do anything to him; for now I know that you fear God, since you have not withheld your son, your only son, from Me."

Then Abraham lifted his eyes and looked, and there behind him was a ram caught in a thicket by its horns. So Abraham went and took the ram and offered it up for a burnt offering instead of his son. And Abraham called the name of the place, The-Lord-Will-Provide; as it is said to this day, "In the Mount of the Lord it shall be provided."

Then the Angel of the Lord called to Abraham a second time out of heaven, and said: "By Myself I have sworn, says the Lord, because you have done this thing, and have not withheld your son, your only son, I will bless you, and I will multiply your descendants as the stars of the heaven and as the sand which is on the seashore; and your descendants shall possess the gate of their enemies. In your seed all the nations of the earth shall be blessed, because you have obeyed My voice." So Abraham returned to his young men, and they rose and went together to Beersheba; and Abraham dwelt at Beersheba (NKJV).

Because of Abraham's obedience, we have a promise passed down to us. God foresees and provides all of our needs. He is an all-knowing, ever-present God who knows the beginning from the end.

He foresaw a long-term need, which was the need for our salvation, and gave His son to die for our sins. In His all-encompassing knowledge, He provides more than salvation. He provides day by day, for our short-term needs. Nothing is too small for God to pay attention to for us. He wants us to include Him in everything we do.

Because He can foresee our needs, He can then provide what is best for us. In providing for us, God wants to know that He is most important in our lives. Do we love God with an all-consuming passion? A passion that allows us to bring our greatest earthly treasure to the altar as a sacrifice? Do we worship in total devotion? Is our determination set in stone, and are we willing to obey immediately, God's way not our own?

When we worship Him in total devotion, He will provide. He promises to provide whatever we need to fulfill His goodwill, and He will do it, according to His riches in glory in Christ Jesus (Philippians 4:19 NKJV).

Jehovah Jireh is our provider. When this sank into my spirit, I found myself in a place where I was willing to withhold nothing from God, willing to sacrifice what I loved, ready to be immediately obedient. The more we are committed to Christ, all other passions take a backseat, and we begin to understand that He is worth our total devotion.

CHAPTER TWENTY-ONE

What's Your Sacrifice?

I was very concerned about finances after Dorian died. I remember asking the Lord, "What do I do now?" We were a two-income family. Was I going to be able to pay the mortgage and utilities? I wondered, but I knew deep down inside that it was going to be okay. I wanted to begin planning to make this happen, but I was so tired, physically, and mentally. All I could say was, "Lord, You handle it."

A couple of months before Dorian died, we attended an estate-planning seminar set up by the church. It forced us to get all of our papers in order and update information. We went down to the State Human Resources office to complete and update Dorian's paperwork for him to retire. Everything was in order. When it came time to make homegoing arrangements, I was able to put my hands immediately on every document I needed.

We went to Kelly and Leak Funeral Home, on Candler Road in Decatur, since, only two years before, they buried my sister, Mary. They made our family feel so at ease. I was in and out in no time. I picked out a casket and signed the paperwork. All the papers were in order, and I was able to give the information needed to make it a smooth transaction. We went to the same cemetery, Hillandale Gardens Memorial, and I was able to locate a plot right next to my sister's grave. I was riding on the wings of an angel; I didn't have to do much thinking.

While at the Human Resources office, updating the paperwork with Dorian a few months earlier, they explained how much retirement pay Dorian would receive each month. He opted for a plan that was a little less each month so that, in the event of his death, I would still receive a small pension. I received a letter telling me that since my husband died before ever receiving his first check, I would collect his full pension amount for the rest of my life.

Jehovah Jireh will provide. It was enough to wipe away the fear of not being able to pay my mortgage and health insurance. Medical insurance was so critical. My medications alone would cost upwards of $3000 a month if I did not have health insurance.

My husband's life insurance check came, and I paid the homegoing expenses and opened an educational fund for Raheem. I now had a little nest egg, or so I thought.

It was April, and the members of the church were to bring a tabernacle (sacrificial) offering to church the next Sunday. This offering was to pay for the building of our new 10,000 seat facility. The Family Life Center, where we were worshipping while they were building the sanctuary, no longer had a mortgage.

The Pastor received instructions from the Lord to pay for the building before we had our first worship service in it. At one of the leadership meetings, a visiting minister spoke about our responsibility to fulfill this mandate. He told us that we could raise the money. He challenged us to come and lay hands on the altar. He said, "Someone will be able to give $10,000." When I placed my hands on the altar, I felt a heat hit the palms of my hands. I had no idea what this meant, nor did I have any idea where I would get $10,000 to give.

I heard the Lord say, "Give $10,000." At this point in my life, I knew when the Lord spoke to me—but $10,000? I did not tell anyone what I perceived the Lord was telling me. On that Sunday morning, my hands were shaking as I wrote the check and trembled even more as I dropped it into the offering basket. I was sure the Lord had spoken to me. I could not have done this on my own. I felt a sense of victory in obedience. My friend Cookie, who didn't believe what God had told me about Dorian's death, was the church's financial secretary. I knew she noticed my offering. Before she could say anything to me, I told her, "God said, do it, and I did."

Verses of Matthew 6:25-26 dropped in my spirit. Therefore, I say to you, do not worry about your life, what you will eat or what you will drink, nor about your body, what you will put on. Is not life more than food and the body more than clothing? Look at the birds of the air, for they neither sow nor reap nor gather into barns; yet your Heavenly Father feeds them. Are you not of more value than they? (NKJV)

The next week, I received a letter from my mortgage company. Seasons Mortgage had sold my loan to Countrywide Mortgage. Countrywide was informing me that they had excessive money in my escrow account. They sent me a refund. I pulled out a check for $3443. I was amazed. I thanked God for his faithfulness.

It was not even a week later that the State Merit System sent me a letter informing me of another insurance policy that Dorian had with his job. Enclosed was account information with another $30,000. I fell to my knees and began to worship

God. God let me know that, as a good steward, He trusted me with His money and that as long as I let money flow through me, He would continue to bless me. Jehovah Jireh provides. He sees our needs, long term, and short term.

CHAPTER TWENTY-TWO

You Can Do Nothing Until You Pray, And Everything is Possible Once You Pray.

The most humbling service is to pray for others, to serve others, and to be an armorbearer to your leaders. Regardless of what I was going through, my focus was on God and His people. He stirred up gifts that I didn't know I had. One of them was intercession. Elder Evelyn Jonas, Chief Intercessor, is a powerful praying woman of God. It was through her leadership that this gift matured. She sent me to the hospitals to pray for sick people. It was through these experiences that I began to develop so much more compassion for people. I surrounded myself with praying people of God, and it built up my faith.

I was "enlarging of my tents" (Isaiah 54:2). Because I had never prayed out loud in front of people, I look at this time as being stretched and prepared. It was easier to pray for people I did not know. I told God that He would have to give me the words to pray that would meet people at the point of their needs. I felt an incredible pleasure as I left each hospital room, totally drained after allowing God to use me.

Through my experiences with Adonai (Master) and being among praying saints, I went to another level of allowing the Lord to have control over my life. I had to get to that point of becoming a bond slave to Christ. I knew prayer was the place to start. Without prayer, I could do nothing.

The Lord instructs through prayer. When I follow the instructions, I am always genuinely blessed. If the Lord gives instructions and I don't obey, I find myself temporarily in the desert. I pray for the day that I will hear His voice and follow His instructions totally and entirely in everything concerning my life.

We cannot second guess whether or not we are hearing from God. In her book, What Happens When Women Say Yes to God: Experiencing Life in Extraordinary Ways, Lysa TerKeurst says, "There's no magic formula for being able to discern God's voice. We can learn to recognize it the way we perceive the voices of those close to us: by knowing Him. When we know Him, we can tell if what we're feeling led to do is from Him or not.

99

Five key questions will help you determine if what you're hearing is from God or not:

Does what I hear line up with Scripture?

Is what I'm hearing consistent with God's Character?

Is what I'm hearing confirmed through other messages?

Is what I'm hearing beyond me?

Would what I'm hearing, please God?"

CHAPTER TWENTY-THREE

S.I.N = Simple Instructions Neglected

Praying to God and hearing His instructions is not always easy. Many times it's because I want His approval for things I want to do. When I don't get the "OK," I question why when it appears to be a good thing. I must keep reminding myself that God knows what's best for me, and I should not neglect His instructions.

I wanted to become a part of MIT (Minister in Training) at my church. I began filling out the application, believing this was a good thing. I thought this was something that would help me grow spiritually. I prayed about it, and the next thing I knew, I was registered to take the Christian Education Teachers

Training. I would not have thought to take that training in a million years.

God said, "You will minister, and I will elevate you. You are a minister." I believed God. Many times we need to keep our conversations with God to ourselves because people will convince you that God didn't say it. I took the seemingly never-ending Christian Education Teacher's Training and began to understand even more how much I needed to study the Word of God. The training was intense.

After receiving the Christian Education Teaching Certificate, I was able to create a training manual designed for the intercessors. Our monthly meeting included lessons in spiritual warfare, praise and worship, and the importance of being an armor bearer.

The first class I taught to a group, other than the Levites, was entitled, "There is Power in the Name of God." It introduced me to all the beautiful characteristics of God. I learned something new each time I taught the class, and each time, God presented Himself to me in a different way. I marveled at His awesomeness.

He kept His promise, and I was licensed as a Minister of the Gospel a few years later.

CHAPTER TWENTY-FOUR

The Peace of God Surpasses All Understanding, Ands Guards Your Heart and Mind

One evening, while making dinner, I received a call from Amira, who said she was stuck in traffic on I-85 on her way home from work. A tractor-trailer had overturned and had the traffic backed up for miles. We chatted a few minutes before she told me that a car stalled in front of her. As she stopped to avoid hitting the vehicle, the car behind her hit the back of her car, causing her vehicle to hit the stalled car.

All three of the cars were in the middle lane of traffic. She called the police and waited for a few minutes. It was taking longer than usual for a response from the police since the traffic backed up for miles. The man in the car in front of her had gotten out to assess the damage. She hung up and got out of her car to speak to the man. That was the last time I talked to her.

From the police report, I envisioned what happened next: As she and the man stood alongside their cars, an inexperienced driver who did not see the stalled vehicles until the last minute tried to avoid smashing into the back of the third car. She decided to go between the cars and the third lane, striking both Amira and the man. The driver didn't stop until the damage to her car caused it to stop. Both of them died on the scene. For leaving the scene, the driver was arrested.

"The driver" turned out to be a 17-year-old high school student. My heart was broken not only for my daughter and the other driver but for the young woman as well. She will never forget this tragic event, where she was responsible for the death of two people. I still pray for her today, some 17 years later.

My grandson, Micah, was just turning five-years-old. I knew that God would provide what I needed, so there was no reason to sue for more than what the insurance would pay. I could imagine what her parents were going through.

Micah's father, Cameron, was in no way an absent parent. My new role as guardian allowed me to help this young man discover and pursue what he saw fit for his life with Micah. As a skilled barber, Cameron was able to establish a very lucrative business and become a popular, sought-after barber in the community.

Amira's homegoing was a true testament to the fact that there is a Jehovah Jireh, a place where provisions are made available. Amira and I worked for the same realty company. Having given birth to Micah at a young age, Amira learned to be responsible. Though she was only 23-years old, she was very organized and had her business in order, including her life insurance.

The company we worked for was so supportive and closed down the entire office so that everyone could attend her homegoing, and they paid for the repast. Amira was young, but she made an impact on the lives of family, friends, co-workers, and church family. Amira's Homegoing was held in the main sanctuary to accommodate the hundreds of people who attended the service.

Bishop William Murphy, the Minister of Music of the church at the time, sang one of her favorite songs, *Praise is What I Do*, and we left the sanctuary celebrating her life to another one of her favorite songs: Kirk Franklin's, *Hosana*.

CHAPTER TWENTY-FIVE

There Are No Coincidences

I contemplated what attorney I should retain to handle my grandson's business with the insurance company for the accident, causing his mother's death. Friends and family gave me referrals, but I couldn't shake the feeling that I was to contact The Cochran Firm. In 2002, I had the honor of meeting the world-famous trial attorney, Johnnie Cochran, before the swearing-in of Shirley Franklin, the first African American/ first female Mayor of Atlanta, Georgia, where our prayer team prayed in the auditorium before the ceremony.

At the risk of sounding insane, I kept my thoughts to myself, until, one day, I happened to mention it to Cookie. She looked at me and said, "You do know that Steve Wilson is an attorney at the Cochran Firm?"

I was stunned; I had no idea that Steve, a young man we watched grow up in the church, was an attorney working with

The Cochran Firm. The very next day, I called The Cochran Firm and asked to speak with Steve. When he came to the phone, I told him who I was, and he said, "I heard what happened, and I was waiting for you to call."

The Cochran Firm handled everything from there, and, when it was all said and done, Micah had an annuity that would set him up financially as an adult.

CHAPTER TWENTY-SIX

Be the Light for Someone Else

The Prayer Council's role was to be available to pray for anyone who requested or required it. When people answered an altar call, for salvation or prayer, our team escorted them to the prayer room where we pray in a more focused, fervent way. If they had any interest in church membership, it was our assignment to enlighten them on how to join.

The Intercessors prayed for the membership, leadership, and the Pastor, as the service was going on. Our prayer room was immediately outside the sanctuary. The Telephone Prayer Ministry was also in action during the worship service, to answer phones and pray with people who would call in for prayer during the telecast. My involvement in the ministry helped me in my time of mourning. Praying for others was part of my healing.

As months passed and the imminent change of leadership was apparent, El Shaddai (Lord God Almighty) took the natural order of things and did something supernatural so that I would know it was Him. I was in a position, once again, that I was qualified only because of God. I had no control, and any ability to perform was strictly through Him.

I had only been on the Prayer Council for a couple of months but was diligently observing the inner workings of the ministry. At a Prayer Council meeting, Debra, who was the Director of the Prayer Council, announced that she was looking for her successor. It was time for her to step down. I had a flashback of fifteen years before when I was hired as the manager of a self-service gas station without any experience.

Tradition had it so that the outgoing director would choose her successor and submit the name to the elder who oversaw the prayer ministry. When she made that announcement, something inside me leaped. I got excited, but I did not know why. I had not been a part of the ministry very long. I told my flesh to sit down.

I wasn't acquainted with the members before becoming a part of the prayer ministry, so I felt like an outsider. It was not because anyone made me feel that way. It was quite the contrary. I was encouraged to attend a fellowship at the home of one of the members. Cynthia, who was the team leader and Debra's assistant, was insistent that I attend. It turned out to be a wonderful time.

I brought my Richard Smallwood and Vision Adoration video and a card game called, The Ungame. It was a set-up by God. The game entailed answering questions from a deck of cards. Each subject was tailor-made for the woman who had to answer. It was a tool that brought an intimacy to the group, and we got to know each other on another level.

Right before the next monthly Prayer Council meeting, I was met by Debra in the hallway. She stopped me as I was about to enter the meeting room and asked if she could speak to me. We walked over to an alcove near the meeting room, out of view of others that might be arriving for the meeting.

She began to tell me that her time as director was up and that she had been praying for God to send someone to fill the position. She wanted to fill the position with someone she believed God had sent. She thought the person was me.

I was speechless. I did not know what to say. Debra told me to pray about it, and I would see that it was God's will. I don't remember anything else that happened that evening. I kept going over and over in my mind the feeling I felt when she first announced she was stepping down.

I then began to think about the fact that I was new and wondered how the group would take it. I speculated how Cynthia would react since she was Debra's assistant. It made sense that she would be the next in line to be the director. It became overwhelming, and I had to release it to God. I had to believe that He knew what He was doing. It had to be Him in control of this situation.

I accepted the position with the blessing of the Elder, and, believe it or not; the transition went better than could be expected. The intercessors who thought that their season in that ministry was over went on to their next assignment. New intercessors came on board. Cynthia, who was sometimes in rebellion but mostly misunderstood because she is radical about God, turned out to be an absolute blessing. She supported me and had my back from the beginning. Cynthia told me that God showed her that I was the one for the position, and her duty was to serve with me. I don't know too many people who could have flowed the way she did. It had to be God! After 25 years, she is still a devoted prayer warrior in my life.

There was a revitalization of the prayer ministry. The elder changed the name of the ministry to the "Levite Priests Prayer Ministry." A whole new chapter had begun.

CHAPTER TWENTY-SEVEN

Intercession is Never Convenient

Under the leadership of the Elder of the Levite Priests, the transition was phenomenal. With instruction, prayer, patience, and obedience, the Levites gained knowledge and power. We began to see the prayers of those who came before us, as well as our prayers, answered.

My desire to pray for the Pastor was overwhelming. Something was going on in his life and with his physical body. I would wake up at 4:00 am, or 5:00 am each morning, urgently knowing that I needed to intercede on his behalf. I mentioned this to two no-nonsense, praying women of God, and, amazingly, they felt the same way. They were praying for him at that time also. We began to pray together, via telephone, at 5:00 am each morning. (This was way before conference calling became available) We lovingly called ourselves "The Pastor's Spiritual Bodyguards."

As an intercessor, God will show you things that you are to pray about privately. We shared the freedom to pray about anything God showed us concerning him without fear of breach of confidentiality.

CHAPTER TWENTY-EIGHT

Follow the Vision

As the newly appointed Director of the Levite Priest Prayer Ministry, I saw God move in so many ways. I was learning more and more about the importance of being obedient to what God would have us to do. The Pastor was a remarkable visionary. The Lord showed him that we needed to pray for the nation. He sent the prayer warriors to Washington, D.C., in 1999, to pray for our country.

Our assignment was to walk around the White House, the Capitol, and the Treasury seven times, praying. There were three buses, each leaving Atlanta strategically to arrive in Washington D.C. at 6:00 a.m., 12:00 noon, and 6:00 p.m. There was no sightseeing, just a fulfillment of our assignment. We prayed and returned to the bus. I remember, as we rode out of D.C., someone pointed out the Pentagon, and we began to pray as we rode almost entirely around it on our way to the expressway.

Next, we were off to New York City. Fifty prayer warriors paid their airfare to fulfill this assignment. We walked around the financial district in the Wall Street area. Our walk ended right before we got to the World Trade Center buildings. Little did we know God had another plan for those buildings.

God truly amazed us by allowing us to end our walk at Trinity Church, a place that stands as a representation of religious piety and devotion within one of the largest business districts in America. According to the church history, "Trinity Church was founded by a charter of King William III of England in 1697. The present building dates back to 1846. The church has truly survived the test of time and has remained, for all intents and purposes, unchanged in a city where the only thing constant is change.

The heavy bronze front doors to the church show an excellent example of the flamboyancy of its neo-Gothic design. The beautiful sandstone face of the church is decorated with Gothic spires and pointed arches and stained-glass windows.

When the church was built, its 281-foot spire and cross were the highest point in New York and dominated the skyline of lower Manhattan. Trinity was a welcoming symbol of hope for ships sailing into New York Harbor during the 19th and 20th centuries. Trinity offered special ministries to meet the needs and hopes of the many immigrants who poured into New York. Trinity has always ministered to the needs of the poor and disadvantaged. In 1705, it was New York City's first ministry to African-Americans, both enslaved and free.

Nuzzled among the high-rise buildings of the Wall Street financial district, St. Paul's Chapel was the church where President George Washington worshipped when New York was the first capital of the United States. The original burial ground at Trinity Church includes the graves and memorials of historical people such as Alexander Hamilton, William Bradford, and Robert Fulton."

We came together in this marvelous place and prayed. The presence of the Lord undoubtedly met us there. God hears the prayers of the righteous and prepares us ahead of time for many things that may happen in our lives. The preparation may be for experiences that will take place next month, next year, or in ten years. We were learning to be sensitive to the Holy Spirit.

Two years after our walk, on September 11, 2001, the World Trade Center Towers were destroyed in an attack by terrorists.

Trinity Church, as well as St. Paul's Chapel and the church's office building, were covered in debris from the bombings but not damaged. These buildings are located directly across the street from the World Trade Center site. St. Paul's Chapel would become the home of an eight-month volunteer relief effort after the terrorist attacks.

I often wonder what might have happened at the World Trade Center if we had not stopped at the Towers' front doors and continued to walk around the Towers or rode entirely around the Pentagon praying? A better question is, what if the Pastor had never given the instruction for us to travel to these places and pray? We learned a lesson in total obedience, following directions, adding nothing and taking nothing away.

CHAPTER TWENTY-NINE

3:00 a.m.
Talk With God

I was becoming more and more sensitive to the Holy Spirit. My best sister-friend, Michelle, who lives in New York City, called to tell me that her brother, Bruce, had died. The tone of her voice alone said, "I need you here." We are such close friends that we call ourselves twins. We were born the same day, the same year. We have always been there for each other whenever life threw us a curve.

Bruce was her only brother. Though Michelle and I have been friends for over 45 years, I only knew Bruce through her eyes. She loved her brother, despite his many years of drug use. He was the only son in their family of four children.

Along with his mother, his three sisters spoiled him. He suffered terribly with asthma most of his life. His drug use added to his health issues. He received a disability check because he was unable to work. For two years, Bruce was recovering from his drug addiction and lived at home with his mother. They lived in the same apartment for over thirty years. People lovingly joked that Bruce's mother was the Governor, and Bruce was the Mayor of that community. Everyone loved them for the care and concern they had for their community.

Michelle, who is also my prayer partner, began ministering to her brother about six months before his death. At the same time, he was in the hospital battling yet another complication of his illness, he accepted Christ as his Savior, and all hell broke loose in his life. It is a fact that when we are not in God's will, Satan does not waste time on us. We are no threat. When we make a conscious decision to do God's will, we become a threat to Satan, and he will do anything to distract us, hoping we will give up on God.

We say things like, "Before I accepted Christ, my life seemed to be easier." That is a lie Satan wants us to believe. A lot of little distractions can sometimes become overwhelming. I heard T.D Jakes call distractions "gnats."

According to Orkin pest control's website, "Gnats are a nuisance since they do not cause major damage to homes. However, gnats may threaten human health should they transport pathogens from their unsanitary development sites. Since fruit flies might contaminate food and fungus gnats can harm potted plants, residents must eliminate potential breeding and developmental sites, since gnats will multiply and create an unclean environment."

That is what the enemy will do if we don't safeguard against the distractions. God never promised that life would be free of trials and tribulations. After Bruce accepted Christ, Satan went to work. Bruce would have to fight to keep receiving a disability check, even though his health continued to deteriorate. The doctor took one last blood test that he would never know the results.

On a Thursday morning, at about 3:00 a.m., Bruce got out of bed and began to clean up his room, even washing his linens and bedspread. His mother said she heard him talking, and she began to listen to what he was saying. He was talking to God.

He said, "God, I do not want to die, but if you want me, I'm ready."

At this point, his mother entered the room to see if he needed help with a treatment for his asthma. The look on his face told her to dial 911. Bruce died on the way to the hospital. Only God knows if the pending test results would be devastating to him and his family. The fulfillment of Bruce's destiny was in his death.

I flew to New York City from Atlanta to be with my friend and her family. I prayed that God would make my assignment clear. My task was to minister to the people. That's all I heard from God.

Bruce's homegoing service was in a church across the street from the apartment complex where they lived. Though they were not members of this church, the Pastor was very gracious and agreed to allow the service to take place there.

He said, "This is a community church. I would like to give every opportunity to people who would not ordinarily come to church a chance to be in the presence of the Lord."

I arrived at the church early and began to pray throughout the sanctuary and vestibule. People began to arrive to view the body. A man came in and appeared to be devastated. I approached him, and the odor of alcohol was overwhelming.

He sat down in a chair, near the guest book, in the vestibule. The story about Bruce's 3:00 a.m. talk with God before his death had spread like wildfire throughout the community. There was only standing room in the church by the time the service began. I began to minister to this man, telling him that Bruce had accepted Christ in his life, so he had gone on to be with the Lord.

At that point, Bruce's cousin, Vivian, who is an evangelist from New Jersey, walked by and heard us talking. She came over to us, and we began to pray with him for his deliverance from alcohol abuse. He began to weep and accepted Christ as his Lord and Savior right there in the vestibule.

The service began. Bruce's friends, one by one, told of his goodness. Every one of them said, in so many words, that Bruce's death was God's way of talking to them, allowing them to clean up their lives and to turn their lives over to God. The Pastor got up to speak and accused the previous speakers of being spiritual bandits because they had already preached his sermon. He went on to bless us with his message. The Spirit of God was moving so mightily that the Pastor had an altar call for salvation.

Twenty-six people accepted Christ as their personal Savior at Bruce's homegoing service. Praise the Lord! In his death, Bruce led more people to Christ than some people will do in a lifetime. People who would not have ordinarily gone to church received salvation, and people who were looking for a church home found one — what a perfect ending to life, and what a beautiful beginning for those who were born again. God is Alpha and Omega.

CHAPTER THIRTY

Obedience is Better Than Sacrifice

O ur church was about to embark on 50 hours of prayer in our new sanctuary. The invitation to attend went out to all the metro Atlanta churches. One church, in particular, was on the west side of Atlanta. The Pastor is white, as well as most of the congregation. The Lord put our prayer teams together to pray. The Levites visited their church one Friday night for one of their worship services, before participating in a midnight prayer vigil. After an hour of praise and worship, the Pastor began to pray for our country. George W. Bush had recently been elected President for the second time.

Looking at the faces in this church, I would be confident in saying that many of the members were republican. The Pastor began to tell a story about an email that he read, where a chaplain was asking his brother clergymen to pray for the

President. He spoke of how the President had a thank-you party for the volunteers who worked on his campaign.

As he was making his rounds of shaking hands and greeting the volunteers, he came upon a woman with her 16-year-old son. The woman told the President how glad she was that a Christian man had become President. The President stopped and addressed the young man. He asked the lady's son if he, too, was a Christian. The boy said he wasn't sure. Though the President's assistants were urging him to move on so that he could greet everyone, he sat down to talk to the young man about salvation.

Now, I found out later; this story was untrue; it was an Internet fabrication. However, something about that story made me recognize that George W. Bush was human. Something made me realize that I, along with thousands of other people, had prayed that the election outcome would be God's will. Though there was a lot of controversy surrounding the election, when it was all said and done, God allowed the result. It was His will.

We as Christians pray for God's will to be the answer to our prayers, but when we don't get the answer we want, then what? We say God didn't God answer our prayers. Is it only when we receive what we desire that we acknowledge God has moved on our behalf. I realized then that it was more important to be obedient to God, more important to do the things God called us to do. It was no longer essential for me to be a democrat or republican follower. It was more important to be a child of God and a follower of Christ.

I realized my reasonable service as an intercessor was to pray for those in the leadership of our country. The President's daughter almost died while having an appendicitis attack. Did I pray for her healing? No.

The Vice President had a serious health scare. Did I pray for him or his family? No.

I had to ask myself if they had been democrats, would I have been on my knees praying for God to be with them? I would have.

All of a sudden, that ideology seemed so wrong. God convicted me, and I began interceding for George W. Bush, his family, and his administration. Though it wasn't popular, our prayer team understood the importance of praying for our country's leaders. I let the President and his wife know that I was praying for them to be righteous in leadership and included a copy of the Prayer of Jabez for the President. For his wife, I sent The Power of a Praying Wife by Stormie Omartian.

I was surprised when I received a thank you card from the President, wishing my family and me well. No, I did not run out and change political parties, but I was at liberty to vote with newfound freedom. If I did not believe in a democratic issue, I no longer felt bound to go along with it simply because I was a democrat. I think that there is no separation of church and state. We need prayer in schools and the government.

An old Chinese proverb says, "Insanity is doing the same thing in the same way and expecting a different outcome." The political climate was terrible then and is even more horrendous today. The atmosphere is much more violent. Blatant disregard for civil and human rights, allegations of voter fraud and election tampering seems to be acceptable. What have we done in the last eight years to make a change to ensure these terrible things don't continue to happen? We continue to do the same things (most times, we do nothing) and expect a different outcome.

Some preachers spew hatred for our country's leadership, talk about the vile things that are allowed to happen, but don't pray for or encourage people to pray for the government leaders and against the spirit of wrongdoings and then take action to do something to make a positive impact. I believe this is a war that must be battled in the spirit, as this is spiritual warfare, and the wickedness is in high places. Praying for our enemies is essential. Identifying who our enemies are and how to fight a spiritual battle is even more crucial.

PART VI

Jehovah Nissi
"The Lord Is My Banner"

CHAPTER THIRTY-ONE

The Lord is Truth

The banner of God is the gathering place to get renewed strength so that we can have victory over our enemies. It reminds us that the Lord and the Truth, which is the Word of God, is our strength.

The best story to explain this is in Exodus 17:9-16. When Israel fought the Amalekites, Moses stood on a hill with the staff of God. Each time he raised the staff, the Israelites gained power and began to win the battle. When Moses' arms got weary, and he lowered them, the Amalekites would start to win. Aaron and Hur placed Aaron on a rock and held his arms up until there was an overwhelming victory for the Israelites. They understood the power of God.

(Exodus 17:15) Moses built an altar and called the name of it, Jehovah Nissi (KJV).

The Amalekites and the Israelites were in a physical war. Many of us will never fight in a war like that. So why do we need to know the God associated with war? It's because, at the cross, our battle became spiritual. If we believe God has control over everything and the enemy's authority eliminated, why do we have enemies? Why do we continue to fight a defeated enemy?

The enemy has no authority, but his power is still intact, and it's as powerful as ever. Why doesn't God simply eliminate these enemies from our lives? Why does He allow them to attack us continuously? I believe that it gives us a more in-depth and constant dependence on God.

Jehovah Nissi allows us to understand that if God has enemies, His enemies are our enemies. God's enemy, the devil, comes with no other purpose but to steal, kill, and destroy, but Christ came so that we could have life abundantly (John 10:10).

The Lord didn't say we would have a life without pain, trouble, sickness, or sorrow. A part of living life abundantly is knowing that there is a place where we can get what we need to withstand the attacks of the enemy. He gives renewed strength and power. God wanted it understood that He would fight the Amalekites (The enemy) from generation to generation (Exodus 17:16).

He told Moses to write it down in the book as a memorial and recounted the event for Joshua to hear as a witness, so there would be no misunderstanding (Exodus 17:14).

Recognizing who our enemies are is first and foremost. Our enemies are our flesh, the world, and Satan.

CHAPTER THIRTY-TWO

The Flesh

What I believe is meant by the "flesh" is our sinful cravings. We all have them and will always have them. Evil desires don't go away when we accept Christ as our Savior or as we grow older to become "mature saints." We learn to deal with these sinful desires by taking God's moral will and understanding that it is through His power that we keep those desires at bay. It's not as easy as it sounds, but a strategic plan will help with our defense against temptation.

(I Peter 2:11) Beloved, I urge you as aliens and strangers to abstain from fleshly lust, which wages war against the soul (NKJV).

(Philippians 4:7) And the peace of God, which surpasses all understanding, will guard your hearts and minds through Christ Jesus (NKJV).

CHAPTER THIRTY-THREE

The World

(John 15:19) *If you were of this world, the world would love its own. But because you are not of this world, but I chose you out of the world, because of this the world hates you (NKJV).*

Negatively, "the world" means "a sinful value structure."

The world structure is organized by attitudes and viewpoints that conflict with God's order, yet everyone is expected to adapt. Deception and persecution are the pair who pressure us into doing things the way the world does things.

CHAPTER THIRTY-FOUR

Satan

(1 Peter 5:8) Be of sober spirit, be on the alert. Your adversary, the devil, prowls around like a roaring lion, seeking someone to devour (NKJV).

Satan is a liar whose strategy many times comes as oppression. According to faiththerapy.org, "Spiritual oppression is an attempt by Satan to make us fear him or what he can do to us."

Satan also has a strategy to make us either believe he doesn't exist or make us afraid of doing God's will. Our enemies are invisible, and their weapons are spiritual, so we must fight spiritually.

(Ephesians 6:10-18) says, *"Finally, my brethren, be strong in the Lord and in the power of His might. Put on the whole armor of God, that you may be able to stand against the wiles of the devil. For we do not wrestle against flesh and blood, but against principalities, against powers, against the rulers of the darkness of this age, against spiritual hosts of wickedness in the heavenly places. Therefore, take up the whole armor of God, that you may be able to withstand in the evil day. And having done all to stand, stand, therefore, having girded your waist with truth, having put on the breastplate of righteousness, and having shod your feet with the preparation of the Gospel of Peace; above all, taking the shield of faith with which you will be able to quench all the fiery darts of the wicked one. And take the helmet of salvation and the sword of the spirit, which is the Word of God, praying always with all prayer and supplication in the spirit, being watchful to this end with all perseverance and supplication for all the saints" (NKJV).*

The flesh, the world, and Satan all have been conquered. Christ's death on the cross crushed Satan's authority, but his power remains strong. It is not, however, stronger than the power of Jehovah. God's grace allows us to share in His victory. As believers in Christ, Christ's death and resurrection protect our success.

(John 16:33) These things I have spoken to you that, in Me, you may have peace. In the world, you will have tribulation, but be of good cheer; I have overcome the world (NKJV).

(Romans 6:8-14) Now if we died with Christ, we believe that we shall also live with Him, knowing that Christ, having been raised from the dead, dies no more. Death no longer has dominion over Him. For the death that He died, He died to sin once for all; but the life that He lives, He lives to God. Likewise, you also, reckon yourselves to be dead indeed to sin, but alive to God in Christ Jesus our Lord. Therefore, do not let sin reign in your mortal body that you should obey it in its lusts. And do not present your members as instruments of unrighteousness to sin, but present yourselves to God as being alive from the dead and your members as instruments of righteousness to God. For sin shall not have dominion over you, for you are not under law but under grace (NKJV).

(Hebrews 2:14) Inasmuch then as the children have partaken of flesh and blood, He Himself likewise shared in the same, that through death He might destroy him who had the power of death, that is, the devil (NKJV).

CHAPTER THIRTY-FIVE

The Banner of God is Truth

F or the character of God to be seen in us, our reliability and integrity should be apparent and shine through. In contemporary times we say, "My word is my bond," but is it? If we are seeking to be like Jesus, then our word will always be the truth. God is truth, and His word is truth.

(John 17:17) Sanctify them by Your truth. Your word is truth (NKJV).

We can have confidence that if we seek to understand and apply God's Word, it will overpower our enemies. Truth crushes the attacks of the enemy. Our application of God's Word will allow us to experience Christ's conquest over the world, flesh, and Satan. The scriptures tell us this.

(2 Timothy 3:16-17) All scripture is given by inspiration of God and is profitable for doctrine, for reproof, for correction, for

instruction in righteousness, that the man of God may be complete, thoroughly equipped for every good work (NKJV).

(Romans 12:2) And do not be conformed to this world, but be transformed by the renewing of your mind, that you may prove what is that good and acceptable and perfect will of God (NKJV).

(John 8:31-32) Then Jesus said to those Jews who believed Him, "If you abide in My word, you are My disciples indeed. And you shall know the truth, and the truth shall make you free" (NKJV).

(Matthew 4:1-10) Then Jesus was led up by the Spirit into the wilderness to be tempted by the devil. And when He had fasted forty days and forty nights, afterward He was hungry. Now, when the tempter came to Him, he said, "If You are the Son of God, command that these stones become bread." But He answered and said, "It is written, 'Man shall not live by bread alone, but by every word that proceeds from the mouth of God.'" Then the devil took Him up into the holy city, set Him on the pinnacle of the temple, and said to Him,

"If You are the Son of God, throw Yourself down. For it is written: 'He shall give His angels charge over you,' and, 'In their hands, they shall bear you up, lest you dash your foot against a stone.'"

Jesus said to him, "It is written again, 'You shall not tempt the Lord your God.'"

Again, the devil took Him up on an exceedingly high mountain and showed Him all the kingdoms of the world and their glory. And he said to Him, "All these things I will give You if You will fall down and worship me."

Then Jesus said to him, "Away with you, Satan! For it is written, 'You shall worship the Lord your God, and Him only you shall serve" (NKJV).

Jehovah Nissi is our gathering place: A place where we can gather our thoughts, devise our plans, become refreshed, receive new revelations, and look up to the hills where our strength comes from (Psalm 121:1). We can access His Word, which is the Truth. The truth is, what will defeat any enemy. Jehovah Nissi is our Banner of Truth.

CHAPTER THIRTY-SIX

Strategic Battleplan for Virtue

Bishop Johnathan Alvarado preached a four-part series titled, Winning at Spiritual Warfare. He said, "In spiritual warfare, we must stand, wrestle, and withstand."

To sum up, what I heard, the Lord saying through him, "to stand" is to be ready, resolute, and stable with focused determination.

"To wrestle" is to be actively engaged, acknowledging the enemy. It also means to be steadfast and unmovable. The enemy's plan of attack is to dislodge us and get us to move out of our secure position. If we get uprooted, the enemy can then steer us in any direction.

"To be wise to deceit," be on the defensive.

"To withstand" is to be resistant to attack, having opposition to assault, resolve in battle, and to be equal or superior in retaliation. It also means to be firm in the evil days. The "evil days" are particular seasons of intense struggle and spiritual engagement of peril, toil, pain, sickness, and disease.

"Standing" is being in a posture of readiness, understanding the attack is going to come and being proactive in preparation. Don't wait until trouble comes to begin to pray. Pray continually and learning the truth through scripture, because we know an attack is inevitable, is proactive. God wants to see that we understand that we can only win the battle if He is with us.

It seems to make sense to plan for anything we want to be successful. We plan meals when we want to eat healthily; we create a business plan if we want our company to be a success; we plan our vacations so that we will have a good time; we have a plan of escape in case of a fire in our home; we take steps to ensure we achieve our goals. Why wouldn't we create a plan to fight for our lives?

Spiritual strategic planning is part of proactive engagement against the attacks of our spiritual enemies. A winning battle always has a strategy. It's essential to acknowledge that the demonic powers exist. The enemy is always watching for an opportunity to subdue us by adversely knocking us out of position. To this end, studying the tactics of the enemy, concerning ourselves, is crucial. Acknowledging our weaknesses and fortifying those entryways that may give access to the enemy to attack is equally important.

Acknowledging our weaknesses (all of them) can be a daunting task, but we need to know all the entryways that could allow the enemy's spiritual attack to hit a bull's eye. We may be ashamed of things other people don't know about us, but it's a door that needs to be acknowledged and secured. Remember, this is a plan which will not come together overnight. God knows all our faults and will help us because it is in His will that we become righteous in all things.

A strategy could be to block, consistently maintain, and guard the door that leads to our weaknesses; otherwise, the temptation will enter. Before we go to bed at night, most of us check all the doors to make sure they are secure. We know the locations of all our entryways.

Once we know all the entryway locations, "abstain from every form of evil " (1 Thessalonians 5:22 NKJV); in other words, don't put ourselves in a position to be tempted. Don't go to the casino if gambling is a weakness. If overeating is a problem, don't go to the all-you-can-eat buffet. If you are a shopaholic, don't go to the mall. Sounds easy, but it's not.

Avoidance of a place or thing that causes us trouble is the right approach in many instances but not always the answer. Sometimes head-on offensive tactics are more realistic. Of course, there will be times we must go to a mall to shop or to a restaurant to eat. A strategic battleplan to avoid the excessive behavior which would lead to destruction would be in order. Perhaps we can shop with our thriftiest friend; or, when eating out, maybe ask the server not to bring bread ahead of the meal; when the gambling fever hits, have a close prayer partner to call on for help. Simple, practical strategies can help keep us on track.

Truthfully, however, to rid ourselves of sin, we first need the desire to close the door to it. The sin is in excessive, detrimental, and self-indulgent behavior. If you honestly look at yourself and say, "I don't want to give up my sin," then ask God to help you with this first step of desiring what He desires for you. He is always faithful.

Gambling was never an issue for me because my strategy has always been to spend no more than $20 in the casino (usually on a cruise ship) or only purchase lottery tickets when the jackpot payout would be an outrageously high amount of money. At one time, all-you-can-eat buffets were all the rage. Overeating was my downfall. There was Shoney's for breakfast, Ryan's and Old Country Buffet for lunch, all you can eat crab legs at the Chinese buffet for dinner. My thought process was to "eat my money's worth" and eat and eat and eat.

As years went by and weight became a hindrance and health issues ensued, my thought pattern changed. I stopped going to these places to eat once I desired to lose weight and eat a healthier diet. An organization I belonged to meets monthly at the Golden Corral buffet. My strategy is to settle on particular items each time and only allow myself to have one plate of food. It was a challenge the first time, but with prayer, each time became more natural.

Because the enemy is already defeated, we can conquer anything that has the potential to turn into unhealthy habits and addictions. When we desire to stop and ask the Lord for assistance, watch how things change. Each of us has to work out our exclusive battle plan to keep us guarded against the enemy. It's important to note that attacks come to those who are on the battlefield for the Lord.

I used to get so angry with my cousin, who discovered he had cancer but refused to stop smoking cigarettes. I talked about how crazy that situation was and how he had so many excuses for why he couldn't stop smoking.

I smoked cigarettes for many years and would say that I enjoyed smoking (a trick of the enemy). A significant ministry opportunity opened up for me, which would have me travel with a team of nonsmokers for four days.

There was no way I could smoke while I was on this assignment. Why was I so nervous? I prayed and asked the Lord to take the desire to smoke away from me, and He did. I didn't smoke that weekend, nor have I smoked a cigarette since that time, some 30 years ago.

I had to realize that it is not that easy for everyone. My cousin was struggling, and I had to devise a strategic plan to come against my critical spirit concerning him. I love my cousin, and all the things I pointed out to him were right, but when he said, "I know what you say is true, but it still hurts to hear."

Immediately convicted that how I was choosing to deal with the situation was not pleasing in God's sight. I had some nerve, when it took me a long time to take medication that would keep me alive and well.

It wasn't what I said; it was how I said it. My quest to be correct, to have the answers and be the go-to girl, I was striving for perfection rather than excellence.

I read somewhere that "A person with a critical spirit usually makes valid points but in an unpalatable manner." Wow. I had to admit that I tended to be very impatient with people who didn't "get it," even after I spell things out. I had to turn this around. I needed some truth, so I searched the Word of God. My battle plan was to pray scripture before speaking to my cousin.

(James 2:13) For judgment is without mercy to the one who has shown no mercy. Mercy triumphs over judgment (NKJV).

(Mathew 7:1-2) Judge not, that you be not judged (NKJV).

God is the only one who can judge with faultless precision. Judgment is obliged to educate and not destroy. My prayer for my cousin is that God gives him the grace He gave to me when I was in that situation. Someone once said," It's better to be kind than right."

Our battle plan will have us: (1) Stand in readiness, be proactive in engagement, steadfast, and unmovable, with focused determination. (2) Recognize that an attack is imminent toward our family and us or anything we love.

Then we need to devise the part of the plan that will enable us to withstand throughout a particular season of intense spiritual engagement. These are the evil days of struggle, trials, tribulation, sickness, and disease.

Strategies should include a support system, your team: prayer partners, family, friends, and church family. The enemy wants to isolate us so that we have no one to encourage us when encouraging ourselves is not enough. The enemy is a master of oppression. Our team will hold up our arms when we get weary. No one can stand and wrestle the match for us or hold us in a position to withstand attacks of the enemy, but our team can encourage us along the way to victory.

A "Strategic Battle Plan of Virtue" is a dynamic way to transform temptation (a bait to sin) into a performance of virtue. Like any other plan, this plan must also be reviewed regularly for optimum results. The truth of God's Word will always be the weapon for successful counter-attacks against all three of our enemies, the flesh, the world, and Satan.

It is so important that we understand that God is the source of truth and that we believe His truth gives us access to His promises. He has promised us many things, but I highlight:

1.Eternal Life - *(John 3:16) For God so loved the world that He gave His only begotten Son, that whoever believes in Him should not perish but have everlasting life (NKJV).*

This scripture has two promises. If we believe that the death of Christ is payment for our sins, we are rescued from eternal death. All sins are washed away, and all guilt removed forever. The second promise in this verse tells us that because Christ rose from the dead, we too can rise from the dead and have eternal life.

2. Limitless Forgiveness - *(Romans 5:20-21) Moreover, the law entered that the offense might abound. But where sin abounded, grace abounded much more, so that as sin reigned in death, even so grace might reign through righteousness to eternal life through Jesus Christ our Lord (NKJV).*

(Hebrews 10:16-17) "This is the covenant that I will make with them after those days, says the Lord: I will put My laws into their hearts, and in their minds I will write them," then He adds, "Their sins and their lawless deeds I will remember no more (NKJV).

There are times our lives when we let our sins of the past bog us down, and we feel as though God cannot forgive some horrendous sin of the past. Plain and simple, this is not true. When those feelings flood us with guilt, remember there is no sin bigger than the fullness of God's grace.

3. Divine Wisdom - *(James 1:2-3,5) My brethren, count it all joy when you fall into various trials, knowing that the testing of your faith produces patience. If any of you lacks wisdom, let him ask of God, who gives to all liberally and without reproach, and it will be given to him (NKJV).*

All we have to do is compare the times we tried to do things on our own with the times we ask for God's guidance to see that we wasted a lot of time and grace trying to do it on our own only to see the situation fail. Developing a dependence on the Lord makes times of uncertainty clear. It is not easy because we have been disappointed by people who have broken promises or let us down.

(Numbers 23:19) God is not a man, that He should lie, Nor a son of man, that He should repent. Has He said, and will He not do? Or has He spoken, and will He not make it good? (NKJV).

We must trust and depend on the Lord every day, in every situation, not just in the enormous traumatic events, but also in the very mundane and minute things of life.

4. A Marvelous Home - *(2 Corinthians 5:6-8) So we are always confident, knowing that while we are at home in the body we are absent from the Lord. For we walk by faith, not by sight. We are confident, yes, well pleased rather to be absent from the body and to be present with the Lord (NKJV).*

Yes, we are sad, even distraught when a loved one passes away, but if they are in Christ, then we should rejoice that they are now with the Lord. Of course, it is easier said than done. What I have come to realize is that my grief is because I miss that person in my life. We must remember the time we had together, be it a long life of a parent /spouse or a short life of a child. God promised an end to death, sorrow, and pain: Isaiah 25:8, Isaiah 60:20, 1 Cor 15:26, Hebrews 2:14-15, Revelation 7:17, Revelation 20:14, Revelation 21:4.

The Lord promised us that He would prepare a place for us. Are we preparing to move into our home of eternity? There should be no fear of the unknown because God is known to us.

Within the names and characteristics of God, we will find many more of His promises. We have access to the promises of God through seeking truth and honoring our covenant with Him. He always fulfills His promises. He is waiting for us to encounter Him by name and live in the Seventh Day, the day that is blessed and sanctified, where we can access the undeniable resources that He has already provided.

About the Author

As a former Atlanta Cable T.V. public access producer / interviewer, Denise was awarded the "Caber Award" for Best Informational Programming. Since joining the team of the HistoryMakers®, the nation's largest African American oral/video history archive in 2006 as a producer/interviewer. Denise has conducted hundreds of oral /video history interviews for the HistoryMakers archive. She is also the Southeast Regional Volunteer Coordinator of Events for the PBS tapings of "An Evening With The HistoryMakers" programming.

With degrees in Business Administration, Denise was named a "Top Ten Business Woman" by the American Business Women's Association for her work as a personal historian who provides the preservation of family histories as a skilled genealogist. As the CEO of Lasting Legacies LLC, Denise has researched and documented more than 400 family history stories by creating uniquely designed family history books for families to pass on to future generations.

Denise volunteers her time as an HIV prevention Counselor teaching, 'What Women Need to Know About HIV/AIDS," to students for college credits. She is a founding Trustee for the Awesome Foundation-Atlanta, which awards one thousand dollar grants monthly to individuals/companies with worthy causes that impact the Atlanta community.

Denise DeBurst Gines is a licensed minister of the gospel with certification in Christian Education.

CPSIA information can be obtained
at www.ICGtesting.com
Printed in the USA
LVHW081317090420
652795LV00011B/120